Philosophical Perspectives of K. Satchidananda Murty

Philosophical Perspectives of K. Satchidananda Murty

P. Boaz

PRINTWORLD
Publishers of Indian Traditions

Cataloging in Publication Data — DK

[Courtesy: D.K. Agencies (P) Ltd. <docinfo@dkagencies.com>]

Boaz, P. (Pusuluri), 1953-

Philosophical perspectives of K. Satchidananda Murty / P. Boaz.

p. cm.

Originally presented as the author's thesis (Ph. D.).

Includes bibliographical references (p.).

ISBN: 9788124606780

1. Satchidananda Murty, K. (Kotta), 1924-2011.
2. Philosophy, Indic – 20th century. I. Title.

DDC 181.4 23

ISBN 13: 978-81-246-0678-0 ISBN 10: 81-246-0678-1

First published in India, 2013

Printed and published by:

D.K. Printworld (P) Ltd.

Regd. office : *"Vedaśrī,"* F-395, Sudarshan Park

(Metro Station: Ramesh Nagar)

New Delhi - 110 015

Phones : (011) 2545 3975, 2546 6019; *Fax* : (011) 2546 5926

E-mail : indology@dkprintworld.com

Web : www.dkprintworld.com

Foreword

HAVING been the last research scholar of Prof. K. Satchidananda Murty, and having his early work — *Hinduism and Its Development* (1947) got published by including his later vision *The Advaitic Notion* (1985) and his *Evolution of Philosophy in India* (1952) as *Evolution of Indian Philosophy* in 2007 under the Andhra University Philosophical Studies series, it would not be inappropriate on my part to write a foreword to his personality and philosophy. Further my doctorate being directed by him on the study of the Upaniṣads, *Bhagavad-Gītā*, *Brahma-Sūtra* and Śaṅkara's commentaries on them was close to his heart and his research subject; and this research work on Murty was carried out under my supervision, during which time I had the privilege of studying some of his works that revealed the many facets of his vision. Dr Boaz deserves appreciation for exploring the life and philosophy of Murty, my guide, mentor and benefactor.

With reference to the personality and philosophy of Murty, it was remarked that he was a class by himself. For me, he was meticulous, time-bound, systematic and committed to profession. When he was in Visakhapatnam, once I was asked to reach him at 5 p.m. to accompany him to attend a meeting in a nearby town. I was late by a minute; and to my surprise, his car left his residence "Andhra Cottage" sharply at 5 p.m., which I saw at a distance. I was appointed as lecturer in Philosophy Department, Andhra University in 1981; and I became his research scholar, he asked me to sit in his "Śāṅkara

Vedānta" classes for the whole of an academic year, covering more than eighty hours in 180 working days, which was top even in those days. Murty's intention was that I should continue Vedānta teaching in the university after him, a rare privilege for those of my social background, as he was aware of Dharmavyādha in the *Mahābhārata*. Murty was a traditionalist at the bottom of his soul, but rationalist in spirit. His intention reflects consistency in academics; and that a person who teaches a subject must be a student of that particular subject in the graduate studies.

His style during the seminars and meetings is known to those who were acquainted with him, but his temperament was balanced. A Vedānta scholar — T.M.P. Mahadevan, a great Buddhist thinker — T.R.V. Murthi, a Marxist writer — D.P. Chattopadhyaya, and many other young philosophy teachers of the country were in his circle of philosophy. The omniscient personality that we see on his face during seminars disappears while in the classroom before the students. He seems to be so humble while delivering a lecture; he keeps either notes or text on the table, conveys the message and points related to the lesson and syllabus. While explaining the lesson, he reads certain passages; and he never brings his philosophy, personality and experiences into the subject matter under discussion in classroom. I saw him sometimes enjoying himself while reading the Śaṅkara's *Brahma-Sūtra Bhāṣya*, to which logic he was an admirer.

The Indian culture for Murty is inclusive in the sense that Islam and Christianity are as much Indian as Hinduism. Similarly Cārvāka, Buddhism, Jainism and Sikhism are as much Indian philosophies as Vedānta. Not only his philosophy, the personality of Murty was "inclusive". When appointments were made in 1981 to the faculty positions in the Philosophy Department, he whispered that a Muslim should also be on the faculty. The Philosophy Department, at his guidance, taught Śāṅkara Vedānta on the one hand, Buddhism on the other as special subjects of study. For the first time in India, "dialectical materialism" as a special subject was introduced and taught about four decades for the postgraduate students in Andhra University. Not only he wrote Far Eastern philosophies in 1976, but a special paper, "Sino-Japanese Philosophies" was added to the curriculum in postgraduate course in philosophy at Andhra University during 1980s. Philosophy departments in India have been looking to the West so far, it was Murty who pioneered to assert that we should also see towards the East. As such even "African Religions and Thought" was introduced during my headship in 1990s.

Murty was a voracious reader in whose personality *vr̥tti* (profession) and *pravr̥tti* (vocation) were harmoniously synthesized. Therefore, family life was least for him; neither he saved his salary nor made money out of his landholdings being the only son of a landlord. I had the privilege of walking in the procession when his body moved to the funeral place in his native village Sangam Jagarlamudi, while on our way a farmer remarked that people who took Murty's lands on lease for cultivation have became "crore-patis", but Murty remained to remember.

True to his name, Satchidanada Murty was an embodiment of truth, intellect and joy; and taught what he believed to be truth *nija bodha rūpaḥ*, as the disciple of Śaṅkara, Hastāmalaka would say. While Murty was on his mission of reading and writing, lecturing and touring, his spouse Mrs Vedavati looked after the family. It is surprise to say that she represents the *karma-kāṇḍa* aspect of Vedic spirit while Murty resembles the *jñāna-kāṇḍa* of the Upaniṣadic vision; both are *kāraṇa janmulu* born with a purpose. Murty was "a man who made an unforgettable impression on those who knew him".

P. George Victor
Vice-chancellor
Adikavi Nannya University
Rajahmundry

Preface

IN this work an attempt is made to present the views and the uniqueness of Prof. K. Satchidananda Murty's philosophical perspective, especially his remarks on Indian ethos, philosophy and Vedānta. As far as possible all the major works of Prof. Murty have been consulted, particularly his earlier works in which his ideas were deliberately and explicitly expressed.

There is also an introduction on the life of Murty with a review of his major works. Chapter 1 on Vedas and Vedānta contains his interpretation of Vedic sentences in the context of changing times. Chapter 2 deals with his remarks on Indian philosophy for the prospective future of philosophy. Chapter 3 is on metaphysics in which the profoundity of Murty's philosophy on man and the transcendent has been described.

Chapter 4 presents the Indian spirit, and tries to clarify certain misconceptions about Indian culture, Hindu ethos and history. Murty unveils here the humanistic approach to understand Indian culture. Chapter 5 contains the social philosophy of Murty in which his "philosophy of inclusiveness" as a method has been presented. Here Murty appears to be primarily a social philosopher. The conclusion of the thesis contains a retrospective study of Murty's "global understanding of philosophy with Vedāntic spirit".

As a whole the text reveals Murty's contribution to global understanding of philosophy by navigating into the neglected areas of philosophy and by adopting comparative method. He is a visionary who interprets philosophy as a tool for peace and argues that philosophy teachers have been the role models for the transformation of society.

Originally being a doctoral thesis, awarded in 2005, I have modified this work in accordance with the suggestions of H.V. Stietencron, University of Tübingen, Germany, to whom I acknowledge my gratitude. I am also thankful to him for recommending the thesis for publication. I am indebted to my research director, P. George Victor, for his kind help in spite of his indisposition and personal attention without whose help I could not have completed the research.

I profusely thank my classmates and lifelong friends — S.D.A. Joga Rao, Department of Philosophy, Andhra University, and K. Srinivas, Department of Philosophy, Pondicherry University, for all their moral support.

I am grateful to K. Ramakrishna Rao, the former chairman of the ICPR, who have collected the comments on the works of Murty and brought out the *Collected Criticism of K. Satchidananda Murty*, from which I have adopted certain sentences and paragraphs. I am thankful to K. Venkateswarlu, former research student of Murty, and a retired professor of politics, Andhra University, for his enlightening reflections on Murty's philosophy. I am also thankful to M.V. Ram Kumar Ratnam of Acharya Nagarjuna University for arranging an interview with Murty.

I am indebted to M. Edward, Principal, ABM Degree College, Ongole, for giving permission to frequently visit the Philosophy Department, Andhra University. I am also thankful to M.V. Krishnayya, former head of the Department of Philosophy, Andhra University, for showing personal interest and permitting me to use the required books from his personal library. Thanks are also due to K. Ramesh, the youngest son of Murty, for providing books that are out of print. My children Sunny and Simmy have been a source of inspiration to continue my academic pursuits that sustained with the love of my wife, Jyothi which I cherish.

Contents

Introduction

Life and Works

Professor K. Satchidananda Murty was born on 25 September 1924 to K. Veerabhadraiah, a religious-minded landlord and his wife Rajaratnamma in the village of Sangam Jagarlamudi near Tenali in Guntur district of Andhra Pradesh, India. The railway line, which connects Kolkata and Chennai on the East Coast of India, passes through the town of Tenali, which is the nearest railway station to Sangam Jagarlamudi.

Etymologically, Satchidananda Murty means "form of truth, reality and bliss". It is the other name for Omniscient, Omnipotent and Omnipresent God, *Brahman* described in the Upaniṣads. During his childhood, it is learnt that his father and grandparents used to call Satchidananda Murty affectionately "Devudiah" or "Devudu" (God) and his friends "Anandam" (joy).[1]

Murty was given primary education at his residence. Sangameswara Rao, a childhood friend of Murty, informed that teachers of different disciplines used to teach him. The other nearer town to Saṅgam Jagarlamudi was Guntur, which was in those days famous for education, where the Lutheran Missionaries from America established a school, hospital and

[1] Veeramachaneni Sangameswara Rao is a neighbour and childhood friend of K. Satchidananda Murty, who shared with me a number of events associated with the life of Murty, when I met him in Sangam Jagarlamudi village on 10 June 2002.

a college. His father, being himself orthodox and spiritual, employed teachers in Sanskrit, Telugu, Hindi and English languages to educate young Murty. Murty records:

> I have the great good fortune of being the son of one, who himself, being a philosopher, inculcated, very early in my life a genuine taste in and love for philosophy. While quite young I was privileged to study under two eminent *puṇḍits* of the old type (*sampradāya vidyā*) from whom I imbibed a deep affection for and knowledge of Sanskritic Culture and Language.[2]

The individual experiences and also one's own psyche will have the influence on the thought of people and also the root cause for the development of one's philosophical vision. Murty writes that not only the physical and social environment, for which condition oneself is exposed, but also the psychological aspects form the basis of a person's philosophy. As early as in 1949, after becoming lecturer in Andhra University, in his book *Evolution of Philosophy in India,* Murty writes:

> . . . the study of a man's character, of his habits and environment provides a clue towards understanding and appreciating his theories and beliefs. Not only it is necessary to study any theory in relation to the socio-economic structure in which it arises, but it is also necessary to pay any attention to the character and personality of the man who puts it *forth.*[3]

As a young boy Murty was a devotee of Hanumān, who was legend of life-long-celibacy and who helped Lord Rāma to bring back his wife, Sītā from Sri Lanka as recorded in the Indian epic, the *Rāmāyaṇa.* The idol of Hanumān was installed in the Venugopala Swāmi Temple, located in the midst of their lands, for which his father was a trustee.

---

[2] K. Satchidananda Murty, *The Rhythm of the Real,* Preface, p. iii.

[3] K. Satchidananda Murty, *Evolution of Philosophy in India,* p. 13.

At the age of fourteen, young Murty got published a book in Telugu language *Hanumad-vijayamu*. Tripuraneni Ramaswamy Choudary, a social reformer and a poet had written the foreword. As a religious young mind, in the same year, Murty got published the *Nāmasaṅkīrtana Mahimā,* which was a translation from Hindi to Telugu. After completing his studies in Hindu College, Guntur, he joined in honours class (philosophy) at Andhra University in 1943.

His childhood work, the commentary on the *Bhagavad-Gītā* started in 1937, was published in 1941 (that runs more than 500 pages in print). It is surprising to see of a person, at the tender age of seventeen, to write such a philosophical and theological book. Subsequently, he became a philosophy professor in the university.

A study of the works of Murty reveals his academic excellence, which was stated by C.R. Reddy, the then Vice-chancellor of Andhra University, on 27 July 1947:

> He is one of our boy prodigies. While quite young, almost in his childhood, he distinguished himself as a scholar in Sanskrit and lectured on themes, connected with Hindu philosophy. *Bhagavad-Gītā* and other sacred books seem to have been in him almost from his birth. At that stage he was a boy prodigy; scholar, no doubt, but also curiosity. . . . On all accounts he was a student of dynamic and creative personality. Since graduation, he has kept up his original research and literary output. Usually prodigies become vain, ostentatious and boastful, but Satchidananda Murty is a man who understands his limitations, while he strives to reach the highest that is possible. . . . I like him; I have both esteem and affection for him, and wish him every success.[4]

[4] Cited from the Introduction by C. Ramalinga Reddy in K. Satchidananda Murty, *The Rhythm of the Real.*

Murty was married to Vedavati Devi, the daughter of his maternal uncle, Jampala Koteswara Rao of Duggirala village, probably at the age of 21, as recollected by Veeramachaneni Sangameswara Rao. The names of the couple — Vedavati Devi and Satchidananda Murty — are unique and classic representing Vedas, those stand for the *karma-kāṇḍa* and the Upaniṣads, those constitute the *jñāna-kāṇḍa* of Vedic literature respectively. Corresponding to the meaning of their names, in real life Vedavati Devi had taken care of the house keeping and day-to-day activity, while Murty pursued his studies, writing, travelling and lecturing.

As early as in 1947, Murty used to call his ancestral house as "Ananda Ashrama" (the abode of joy), which is evident from the Preface to his book, *Hinduism and Its Development*; subsequently it is found that "Aparajita" (unconquered) replaced it. A glance at his profile reveals the fact that Murty was a committed scholar and teacher at the core of his heart throughout his life, being free from family duties, problems of life and management of the family. He stated this in 1971 by dedicating his book *The Realm of Between* to his wife:

> I have great pleasure in inscribing this book to the person who for over twenty years now has enabled me to be free from all domestic cares, as earlier I was kept free from them, thanks to another person, my father.[5]

After working as lecturer in Tirupati for an academic year and later in Mayurbhanj, Murty came to Andhra University in 1949, as a lecturer in philosophy. He was close at heart with the luminaries of the university. Murty remembers the earlier days of his campus life:

> In July 1949 when P.T. Raju left Andhra for the Professorship at Jaipur, on the recommendation of

[5] K. Satchidananda Murty, *The Realm of Between*, Preface, p. xv.

> Professor Sen, C.R. Reddy appointed me as a Lecturer. When I joined as a teacher Reddy was the Vice-chancellor, and V.S. Krishna was the Principal. I was teaching Logic and Theory of Knowledge and Contemporary Western Philosophy till 1954; from then on till the later sixties Advaita Vedānta, Early Indian Philosophy and Contemporary Western Philosophy, substituting the latter with Systems of Indian Philosophy occasionally; and in the seventies Buddhist hilosophy and Advaita Vedānta.[6]

Established in 1932 the Department of Philosophy, Andhra University, has been a centre for specializing Vedāntic studies. Saileswara Sen, the founder of the Philosophy Department, was a profound scholar in Advaita Vedānta and a specialist in Navya-Nyāya and Symbolic Logic. Murty continued the tradition and contributed for a global understanding of philosophy with Vedāntic vision. When Saileswara Sen died suddenly in 1954, Murty was made the Head of the Department of Philosophy. Though left on certain assignments, Murty led the Department for thirty years till his superannuation in the year 1984. Apart from teaching the systems of Indian philosophy and Western philosophy with special courses on Buddhism and Vedānta, contemporary philosophies have been on the philosophy curriculum in the Department. In early 1960s, as head of the Department of Philosophy, Murty saw that "Dialectical Materialism" has been introduced as a special course in MA programme, and in 1981 the philosophies of China and Japan have been introduced for the first time in India as "Far Eastern Philosophies". As a teacher Murty was cordial to his students, and always careful

[6] K. Satchidananda Murty, "Andhra University: From the Reminiscences", in *Andhra University Golden Jubilee Celebrations Souvenir 1926–1976*, Visakhapatnam: Andhra University Press and Publication, 1978, p. 82.

about the lecture, used to keep the teaching notes on the table while teaching; and he used to foretell about his programmes to the students, so that nobody will miss the other.

For academic discussions and exchange of views a research forum called "Saturday Club" was started when V.S. Krishna was Vice-chancellor of Andhra University. And Murty was made its first secretary, whose duty was to conduct meetings on every Saturday evening by inviting a renowned senior faculty member for exchange of views. Murty enjoyed the fellowship of *puṇḍit*s — D. Venkataramana Sastry, Kolluru Somasekhara Sastry and K. Ramanujacharyulu — who were authorities on Telugu *vyākaraṇa,* Advaita Vedānta and Sanskrit *vyākaraṇa,* respectively.[7]

Murty, for a long time, was the Chairman of Indian Philosophical Congress and Vice-president of the International Federation of the Philosophical Societies. The Government of India bestowed upon him the highest honours Padma Bhushan/Padma Vibhushan by Government of India and many universities in India and abroad conferred on him the Honorary Doctorates — DLH (Andhra, Venkateswara, Nagarjuna Universities, and Sophia University (Bulgaria)).

During the early phase of his academic life from 1938 to 1959, a decade at his native place and another in the university campus, Murty had evolved himself as a person with noble ideas and rational outlook in understanding and interpreting Hinduism and Philosophy in his own way. Starting with the publication of *Hanumad-vijayamu,* he had an academic track of twenty years until the publication of *Revelation and Reason in Advaita Vedānta* in 1959. During this period, apart from the book, *Karu-mabbulu* (Thick Clouds) that contains essays on

[7] K. Satchidananda Murty, "Andhra University: From the Reminiscences", in *Andhra University Golden Jubilee Celebrations Souvenir 1926–1976,* Visakhapatnam: Andhra University Press and Publication, 1978, p. 83.

philosophical and social issues, his other Telugu books cover the devotional and Vedāntic theology. His English works *Hinduism and Its Development* (1947) and *Evolution of Philosophy in India* (1952) speaks of his penetrating interpretation of Hinduism and Indian philosophy on the basis of anthropological and historical facts. While *Thought and the Divine* (1951) contains metaphysical and theological issues discussed by Western philosophers, *The Rhythm of the Real* (1951) speaks of his masterly interpretation of Western philosophical concepts from the standpoint of Indian philosophy. Finally his PhD thesis "Revelation and Reason in Advaita Vedānta" (1959) reveals the comprehensive approach of Murty. As a whole these books speak of the enormous research Murty had done by studying Western philosophy, Indian history and the classical sourcebooks of Indian culture. The scientific outlook, the method of comparison, the dialectical approach on application of facts with the ideals and his vision of Indian culture and philosophy, that formulated and evolved during this period have continued, developed and sustained in his later works also.

In the second phase of fifteen years, which covers from 1960 until he became the Vice-chancellor of Sri Venkateswara University in 1975, Murty had developed academic interaction with various scholars of eminence. He was nominated for coordinating, editing and bringing out a volume on *Religion and Philosophy of the Telugu Encyclopaedia* (1963). In this herculean task, Murty has obtained articles in Telugu language from the teachers of philosophy in India and abroad, which shows his expanded philosophical horizons. He co-authored with A.C. Bouquet of Cambridge for a book, *Studies in the Problem of Peace,* in 1960. In this period without being affected in his personal research, Murty became a social philosopher with global perspective by editing prominent books, assisted by teachers of other departments. His edited works — *General*

Education Reconsidered (1963), *Readings in the Indian History, Politics and Philosophy* (1967) and *Current Trends in Indian Philosophy* (1972) — contain inclusive philosophical concern on the public issues of the society. The *Indian Foreign Policy* (1964) and *Indian Spirit* (1965) speak of his patriotism, fact-speaking nature and the need for the expansion of our perspective towards understanding philosophy. *Metaphysics, Man and Freedom* (1963) and *The Realm of Between* (1974) contain Murty's views on metaphysics and philosophy of religion with reference to human experience in which he has expressed his own original ideas. *Nāgārjuna* (1971) is written as an assignment given by the National Book Trust, New Delhi, which is meant for the general reader. Though the philosophy teachers of India believe that the Indian thought is the best, yet some had the leaning nature to bend their mind towards the West. With the publication of his *Far Eastern Philosophies* (1975), Murty made an attempt to turn the attention of the philosophical world of India to the East, believing that neither philosophy nor spirituality is the monopoly of any country or any culture.

The last phase of the academic life of Murty is spread over another twenty years, starting from 1976 to 1995 in which he wrote wonderful dissertations, *Indian Philosophy since 1498* (1982), *The Advaitic Notion* (1985) and *Vedic Hermeneutics* (1993). In these works, without any hesitation he draws conclusions on the thought of Gandhi and Ambedkar and the implications of the metaphysics of Vedānta in real life in the society. *Philosophy in India* (1985) and *Radhakrishnan: His Life and Ideas* (1989) are the major research works in this period. The former records not only the history of philosophy in the past but also visualizes how philosophy should be taught in the universities in future; the latter, co-authored with Ashok Vohra, meant to extol philosophy through the life of a philosopher.

Having been worked as Vice-chancellor of Sri Venkateswara University for three years, Murty came back to Andhra University in 1979, and devoted his life for research and teaching. After superannuation in 1985, Murty left to his native village Saṅgam Jagarlamudi, and then left to New Delhi in 1986 to stay there for three years as Vice-chairman, University Grants Commission. After coming back from New Delhi, Murty stayed at his native place for two decades, reading and writing. He came to Andhra University and delivered talks, probably the last lectures, for four days from 14 to 17 December 2000 on the "Perennial Ideas of the Ages" to mark the turn of the twentieth century. Subsequently until his death on 24 January 2011, he lived like a religious reclusive in his ancestral house in Sangam Jagarlamudi, ceasing to interact with people, sometimes even not allowing his admirers to see his face.

REVIEW OF LITERATURE

During his life of eighty-six years (1924 to 2011) Murty had spent fifty-five years of active academic life, which is not possible for any other university professor in this country. His contribution to philosophy is well known among the philosophers in India and abroad. Murty had started his philosophical career by writing books from the age of fourteen. Teaching philosophy from the age of twenty-two, he continued his pedagogic skills even after his superannuation. In Telugu he authored five works, translated five and edited a volume for the *Telugu Encyclopaedia*. In Hindi he edited *Contemporary Indian Philosophy*. In English Murty edited four books, translated the *Sad Darsana Samuccaya of Haribhadra* and co-authored *Radhakrishnan: His Life and Ideals,* apart from being the author of eighteen prominent titles, of which some are briefly discussed below.

HINDUISM AND ITS DEVELOPMENT (1947)

Written at the age of twenty-three, this book contains a series of five lectures delivered at the S.V. College, Tirupati, on the invitation of Gopati Narayanaswamy Chetti, President of the College Committee of the Tirumala Tirupati Devasthanams. Each lecture constitutes a chapter in the book.

Probably influenced by the Second World War, Murty pointed out in his first lecture on spiritual vision, the "global outlook" as the solution for everyday problems. In the second lecture, he proposed the spiritual vision of life to satisfy the needs of man rather than the religious rituals and dogmatic beliefs. The third lecture on Vedānta contained the metaphysical doctrines of the Upaniṣads, bringing their significance for man in the world. In the fourth lecture he emphasized that the religious practice is nothing but the assertive life of righteousness. The racial element in the evolution of caste system in India was theorized in the fourth lecture apart from a discussion on the Hindu view of life-stages. The final lecture, which covers half of the book and in nine sections, traced the evolution of Hinduism. To meet the intellectual desires of the age, in the words of Murty "a reorientation of the fundamental problems of life and moral reconstruction of the world" is needed. Thus an attempt is made to trace the historical and doctrinal, chronological and logical evolution of Hinduism from the time of Indus Valley Civilization to the modern age of Aurobindo, Tagore and Mahatma Gandhi, by interpreting the influence of the Mughals and the British on Indian history.

THOUGHT AND THE DIVINE (1951)

This book showcases Murty's acquaintance with the Western philosophy. The first two chapters are on the Greek philosophers — Plato and Aristotle — and the other three chapters are on the theologians of the middle ages — St. Augustine, St. Anselm and St. Aquinas.

Murty has described the thought of the philosophers and theologians by comparing and contrasting with Indian thought based upon the original texts. Thomas Aquinas' proofs for the existence of God and the nature of God have been brought out systematically. The idealism and the phenomenalism of Berkeley and Hume have also been highlighted, respectively. The noteworthy feature of the book is the systematic treatment of the subject and the logical analysis of the topic, which has been neglected by Indian writers of philosophy.

THE RHYTHM OF THE REAL (1951)

This is a book written before 1947, which is evident from the introduction written by C. Ramalinga Reddy, the then Vice-chancellor, Andhra University, but published in 1951. A work of 150 pages, it contains five chapters on five concepts with critical scholarship based on the philosophies of East and West. Prof. Gilbert Ryle of Oxford University, to whom the book is dedicated, has read the entire typescript and made appropriate suggestions. This work is a standing evidence of the author's profound erudition in both Indian and Western philosophies, and deals with the following concepts in separate chapters.

1. *Beauty*: The meaning and definition of beauty has been analysed in relation to Indian terms, *sundara* and *rasa*. The view of Western philosophers and poets including the Indian point of view has been discussed.

2. *History*: This chapter signifies the meaning and importance of history, evolution of European history and the Greco-Roman conception of history. The Biblical perspective of God in history found place in it.

3. *Causality*: Bringing forth the causation theory, Murty discusses the problem of cause and effect with reference to Nyāya and Advaita systems of Indian philosophy along with few related remarks from Buddhism.

4. *God*: The conception of God and the proofs for the existence of God are narrated with reference to Western and

Indian philosophers. The Indian point of view based on Śaṅkara and Rāmānuja on the one side and Sāṁkhya system on the other side are found place in this long essay.

5. *Good*: Similar to the above chapter, comparing the Western perspectives, the concept of good has been discussed on the basis of Indian tradition, especially the Vedāntic views.

EVOLUTION OF PHILOSOPHY IN INDIA (1952)

In this book of 281 pages, written at the age of twenty-eight, Murty, as a young man, traces the evolution of philosophy in India with reference to socio-political and economic conditions.

As a whole the first five chapters of this book deal with the socio-political, geographical and racial causes for the formation of Indian thought and its development. The next five chapters are devoted in detail about what is philosophy and Indian philosophy including the Vedas and Upaniṣads. The other ten chapters are devoted for the heterodox systems — Lokāyata, Jainism and Buddhism of Indian philosophy. This book does not contain any chapter or section on the systems of Nyāya, Yoga and Mīmāṁsā. Probably Murty might have been influenced by the writings of Max Müller, Paul Deussen and Garbe, assuming that the Mīmāṁsā as scriptural exegesis of the ritualistic portion of the Vedas, Yoga as a form of discipline of meditation and Nyāya as the science of logic having little philosophy. A.R. Wadia, the then Pro-Vice-chancellor of MS University, Baroda, in his foreword to this book remarked "the standpoint taken up is something fresh and original even to the extent of being unconventional for an Indian".[8]

In his introduction to this book, the great son of India M.N. Roy has asserted that the philosophical heritage of India has to be discovered and properly evaluated. He congratulated

[8] A.R. Wadia, in his Foreword to K. Satchidananda Murty, *Evolution of Philosophy in India*, p. v.

the author by saying that "these chapters are of great importance methodologically, and as such constitute the more valuable part of a commendable work of scholarship".[9] A second edition of this work with a new title, *Evolution of Indian Philosophy*, has been brought out in 2007 being edited by his younger colleagues and formerly research scholars — P. George Victor and V.V.S. Saibaba.

REVELATION AND REASON IN ADVAITA VEDĀNTA (1959)

A masterpiece of Murty's scholarship, this research work is his PhD thesis, divided into two books, each containing two parts and printed in more than 300 pages. As a whole the chapters are twenty-three in total with more than 1,000 references from classical Sanskrit texts and translations. If one opens the book, one will find a glaring quotation of Mallinada, which reminds of Murty's standpoint, which implies that all the exposition is interpretation of classical texts and nothing was new.

The first part of the book contains an exposition of the conceptions and interpretation of Veda on the basis of Advaita Vedānta. The second part expounds the relationship between the Veda and perception, and the function of reason with reference to *Brahman* knowledge. Part three relates to the criticisms of Mīmāṁsā and Nyāya against Advaita Vedānta. The last part of the text deals with the conceptions of God and revelation on the basis of the Vedāntic scriptures, as interpreted by the Western thinkers.

According to Sengaku Mayeda, this book prominently reflects three features: (1) sharp critical mind, (2) wide and deep knowledge of Indian philosophy in general, and (3) that

[9] M.N. Roy, in his Introduction to K. Satchidananda Murty, *Evolution of Philosophy in India*, p. vii.

of European philosophy.[10] In the *Philosophical Quarterly,* C. Kunhan Raja commented:

> In this Murty has for the first time . . . thrown a challenge to some of the philosophical doctrines maintained in the Advaita Vedānta system as fundamentals. A bold step. . . . A very lucid and comprehensive presentation of the problems of God and Revelation as developed in the Advaita system. . . . The problems are presented without prejudice, in a very impartial way, based on authoritative texts. . . . The criticism of the Advaita Vedānta standpoint and the presentation of the author's own views are contained in the Second Book. The author applies strict logic to substantiate his position.[11]

THE QUEST FOR PEACE (1960)

Originally published as *Studies in the Problems of Peace* in 1960 with A.C. Boquet of Cambridge, as co-author, this work was reprinted in 1986, containing only those parts written by Murty. This book, exclusively devoted to political philosophy, is divided into seven chapters. The first chapter is on the Hindu perspective of punishment and duty. The second chapter covers Hindu ideology relating to ruling class, and the rules and codes of administration. The third chapter, which is on non-violence and forgiveness, traces their roots in Jainism, Buddhism and Christianity, and provides the base for Gandhian thought.

The fourth chapter is on violence and terror, and traces out their roots in the history of Greek and Roman empires. The terrorist practices in the medieval and modern Europe,

---

[10] Cf. Sibajiban Bhattacharyya and Ashok Vohra (eds.), *The Philosophy of K. Satchidananda Murty,* p. 122.

[11] Cf. K. Ramakrishna Rao et al. (ed.), *Collected Criticism of K. Satchidananda Murty,* p. 44.

including Fascism and Nazism have been noted. The fifth chapter is on liberty and revolution, and narrates the modern schools of thought from the standpoint of Russell, Locke, Jefferson and Karl Marx. The evolution of Communism and the "theory of state" are discussed. The sixth chapter is about various theories and causes of war with a hope to live without war in order to attain peace. The seventh chapter is made out for peace. Revealing certain ideals inculcated in the ancient Greek and Roman empires, and in Christianity and by kings like Aśoka, the concepts of human brotherhood and tolerance have been thoroughly dealt with.

The Epilogue, which may be considered as the last chapter, contains Murty's vision to realize peace through the society of scientists, intellectuals and philosophers, the *Republica literaria.*

P.V. Narasimha Rao, the former prime minister of India, who wrote the introduction to this publication, states that it covers "a wide panorama of human civilization and deals with the concept as well as the research for peace in all its ramifications".[12] Narasimha Rao advocates that in order to attain peace, even in one self, there should be equality in the society.

METAPHYSICS, MAN AND FREEDOM (1963)

Containing the three lectures, delivered at Annamalai University in 1960, this book reveals the original ideas of Murty. The first lecture was presented originally in a seminar at the University of Chicago in 1954. The last two lectures have been partly discussed and presented in the Proceedings of the International Congress of Philosophy held at Venice in 1968 and in the IXth Session of the Pakistan Philosophical

[12] Cf. K. Satchidananda Murty, *The Quest for Peace*, Introduction, p. x.

Congress held at Rajshahi in 1962. S. Radhakrishnan in his foreword to this book remarks:

> Those who deny metaphysics do so as a result of a metaphysics, which is not aware of being one. Each of us should have a reasoned faith to live by.[13]

In the first lecture, which can be called as the introduction on metaphysics, Murty details the origin and meaning of metaphysics apart from the need for metaphysics. The second lecture is on the various approaches towards understanding man. Some of the ideas of this lecture contain man and individuality and dualism of the self and body, drawing inspiration from the doctrines of Western philosophy and the schools of Indian philosophy. Murty advocates the unity of self and body even for the seekers of transcendence.

The third lecture is on the concept of freedom, which described as the effect of human reason, thinking in a reversal way contrary to the human conditions of the present life. According to some schools of Indian philosophy, freedom can be attained in this very life while living in the society.

INDIAN FOREIGN POLICY (1964)

This book is written during the time when India's relationship with its neighbours is at stake. In it Murty describes the Indian foreign policy, sharing the expectations, identity and demands of a nation, which is emerging as the world's largest democracy. This book is divided into three parts. Part one is on ideological moorings in which Murty describes the views of Kauṭilya in *Arthaśāstra* and the views expressed in *Manusmṛti* and *Mahābhārata.* He also brings out the other concepts evolved on the basis of the doctrines in Jainism and Buddhism. The attitudes and factors responsible for the formation of Indian

[13] K. Satchidananda Murty, *Metaphysics, Man and Freedom,* p. ix.

foreign policy, the nature and implication of the non-alignment concept have been explored. Murty says:

> Peaceful co-existence is possible on the basis of mutual respect and co-operation without any assertion for seeking for what is to be considered as to be truth or right.

The second part deals with some specific issues with reference to military-action in Goa, which was a Portuguese colony on Indian soil, and India's relationship with China and Japan. In the third chapter entitled "Discussion and Evaluation" Murty proposed some suggestions for re-orientation of foreign policy with the formation of a body of advisors consisting of historians, philosophers, political thinkers and cultural anthropologists for advancing the external affairs. He also advocated the introduction of "area studies" in the universities in order to help the government in policy formation.

The annexe of this book brings forth some of the penetrating thoughts of the ancient texts, Aśoka and Gandhi. The relation between ethics and politics, the need for peaceful co-existence of nations has been asserted when the world was divided into blocs.

THE INDIAN SPIRIT (1965)

This book is an Indian philosophy teacher's response to the Western scholar's misconceptions about India, and reflects the Indian mind, revealing what India stands for. The first chapter denounces the Western criticism of India as land of mystical and world-negating attitudes and stagnant society. Murty proposes the positive attitude of life described in the ancient Indian scripture, practices of Indian culture, and the evidences of Indian genius narrated in the past and present.

The second chapter on Indian perspective of history is a response to the criticism of Amaury de Riencourt's arbitrary remarks about Hindu Atavism. Hindu perspectives of culture, history and social ethics are the content of the third chapter. The Greek image of Indian philosophy constitutes the fourth chapter, in which the grandeur of Indian thought, which influenced and reached the West, has been discussed. Chapter five is on philosophical thought in India, expounding philosophy as the "science of review", "science of salvation" (*mokṣa*) and "science of interpretation". The importance of common sense, freedom of will, the uniqueness of soul and its destiny, and the ideal perspective of Hindu life are discussed. According to Murty, "transcendental materialism" is the unique contribution of the Indian philosophy, which according to him is both spiritual and materialistic, thus forms the sixth chapter. Karl Potter's charges against Indian philosophy are critically evaluated in the annexe of this chapter. In the seventh chapter a brief discussion on the nature of religion and ethics in Hindu culture is done. The last chapter is about the origin and nature of political ideas in Hindu literature.

NĀGĀRJUNA (1971)

Nāgārjuna was a great organizer of Mahāyāna Buddhism. In metaphysical profundity, logical acumen and spiritual insight, among Indian thinkers he has no equal except Śaṅkara. He is one of the greatest philosophers that the world has known. The Indian and Tibetan traditions speak of Nāgārjuna as a tāntric, and according to early Chinese accounts, he was a mystic of high attainments. In fact Buddhists of China, Japan and Tibet considered him to be the second Buddha who once again set in motion the "Wheel of Dharma" (truth and righteousness).

This book on Nāgārjuna by Murty, which is divided into two parts, contains ten chapters and printed in 117 pages with selections from Nāgārjuna's works, *Ratnāvalī* and *Mādhyamika-*

śāstra. One finds here not only the interpretation of Murty, but also the tremendous treatment, through out the book, about the philosophy of Nāgārjuna. Murty discusses about the Buddhist sources for Nāgārjuna's biography, which can be divided into *siddha* accounts, histories, the scriptures and biographies. Murty is to somehow accept the writings of Hsuan Tsang. According to him King Sātavāhana treated Nāgārjuna with great respect and kept a guard of honour at his residence and built for him a great monastery spending nine crores of gold coins.

Nāgārjuna's philosophy avoids the extremes of affirmation and negation — "is" and "is not". It does not affirm that there is substance or self, nor does it deny them. Here Murty narrated the views and philosophy of Nāgārjuna, giving explanation vividly as and when required. He says that when *dharma* is properly practised, it first produces happiness and prosperity (*abhyudaya*) and then salvation or liberation. The practice of *dharma* is summarized as faith and insight.

THE REALM OF BETWEEN (1973)

Having four chapters on (i) suffering, (ii) salvation, (iii) religious action, and (iv) transcendental philosophy, this book is a revised version at Murty's lectures on the philosophy of religion delivered at Manchester College, Oxford, and the University of London in 1962.

This book is mainly about the middle-state between What-is and the Holy, or the realm between the transience of things and the truth of things. The first chapter deals with man's condition: suffering, evanescence and finitude; and the second considers the possible ways of escaping this condition. Murty says that a good deal of suffering could be eradicated by radically transforming the society through rational human action. Salvation is the experience with certitude of peace, security and contentment.

The third chapter expounds the two basic forms of religious action — sacrifice and worship. Sacrifice is said to be giving up of what one has, which leads to transformation of life; while worship is taking refuge in God with a thought that He is the only way to salvation. The fourth chapter grapples with the questions of God's existence, non-appearance, silence, absence and death, and the dialectics of atheism and the relation between religion and ethics. Murty remarks that atheism does not necessarily lead to the deification of man or history, or to immorality; nor is it true that "there is no virtue if there is no immortality". Without belief in God or immortality some can live, endure and find meaning in life and engage themselves in ethical endeavours of the highest type, says Murty. In this context Sunit Kumar Chatterjee's remarks are worth reading:

> I have found by listening to Murty's talks that I can follow his language — and that there is in his talks a sort of perception of the value of the great Myth that is God; and that one without being a philosopher can find some pleasure, some *bhāvavilāsa* or superficial aesthetic spiritual joy, from the *prasaṅga,* the *upanyāsa* — the illustrative discourse on a great theme — that he makes. I . . . find Murty's talks stimulating, to say the least. . . .[14]

FAR EASTERN PHILOSOPHIES (1976)

A book on the philosophies of China and Japan it is a unique attempt of an Indian philosopher for the first time, when the Indian universities had never entertained courses on the philosophies of China and Japan and when the Indian philosophy teachers were leaned towards the West only. This book is based on the lectures delivered at Mysore University and published by it in which 100 pages are devoted to the philosophy of China and another 90 pages dealt

[14] Cf. K. Ramakrishna Rao et al. (eds.), op. cit., p. 213.

with the philosophy of Japan. Murty, while narrating the concepts, has compared the basic principles of Chinese and Japanese philosophies with the similar views found in Indian culture and philosophy.

Among the three chapters devoted to Chinese philosophy, the first chapter details the origin of the six schools of Chinese philosophy and the development of Buddhism in the context of Chinese history and society. A number of traditional schools, views and concepts of primitive Chinese wisdom are given. Murty, in the second chapter, discusses the Literati School of Chinese philosophy with reference to Confucius, Mencius and others. The third chapter is on the philosophy of Lao-tzu, who propounded the School of the Way or Taoism.

The fourth and the fifth chapters are on the Japanese philosophy, detailing Japanese creativity, their culture and aesthetic sense. A discussion on Zen philosophy and application based on meditation is dealt in the former chapter, while the origin and development of Shinto philosophy and the associated concepts are detailed in the later chapter with a brief sketch on divine rule and the later schools of Shinto philosophy.

INDIAN PHILOSOPHY SINCE 1498 (1982)

According to Murty:

> Justice is done to a philosophy only when it is analysed, evaluated and critically assimilated; defecation and eulogization of any thinker — whether Śaṅkara or Gandhi, Marx or Wittgenstein — is not the best way of paying a tribute to them.

Based upon this precept, Murty wrote the *Indian Philosophy Since 1498,* when Vasco da Gama found the sea route to India, which was cause for the arrival of new ideas and to spread the flavour of Sanskrit philosophical works to the West. In this book Murty evaluated the philosophies of Mahatma

Gandhi, Radhakrishnan and Ambedkar, who have influenced the Indian mind, tremendously in the twentieth century.

The first chapter of the book is an introduction in brief about the philosophical activity during sixteenth–nineteenth centuries in India. The second chapter is devoted to show how socio-economic changes cause changes in religious and philosophical conceptions. Murty adds in the second chapter the prominence and influence of Islam and Christianity, and discusses the contribution of Muslims and Christians in the eighth and ninth chapters, respectively. The third, fourth and fifth chapters contain a critique of Gandhian thought, where the influence of Indian traditional concepts and values on Gandhi has been traced. The Gandhian programmes of non-violence and *satyāgraha,* his ideas on democracy, *Rāma-rājya* and economy have been dealt with critical appraisal. Radhakrishnan's conception of philosophy and his thought find a place in the sixth chapter. As a whole the book is historical and critical, informative and innovative, while bringing certain issues of our time forgotten by the writers of contemporary Indian philosophy.

PHILOSOPHY IN INDIA (1985)

Philosophy in India is a book on the history of philosophical tradition, teaching and research in India, originally submitted to the Unesco in the year 1982 and revised subsequently for the Indian Council of Philosophical Research (ICPR). This book details the general philosophical situation in different regions of the country, assisted by a number of philosophy teachers. With more than 200 pages in print, the text is divided into seven chapters.

The first chapter contains the meaning and role of philosophy in Indian culture. The second chapter traces out the history of philosophical thinking with reference to the heterodox and orthodox schools of Indian philosophy; and Murty points out the need for the interpretation of Indian philosophy in the context of social, political and economic circumstances. Murty for the first time reveals to the philosophic community about the philosophical contribution made by saints, mystics and *gurus* of medieval India, in the third chapter.

The fourth and fifth chapters contain the contributions made by some of the Hindu reformers and university professors to philosophy in modern India, and also the present situation in the philosophy departments throughout the country, detailing the courses of study and the nature of research that has taken place. Not only the problems of the philosophy teachers in their profession in attracting the better students have been discussed, in the sixth chapter, but also suggestions made by philosophy teachers for the rectification of philosophy in India are added. The last chapter catalogues the goal and nature of philosophical teaching, the social relevance of philosophy; and the appropriate curriculum to be adopted is discussed as an agenda for the future.

THE ADVAITIC NOTION (1985)

The Advaitic Notion is an address delivered in the presence of H.H. Jagadguru Sri Bharati Tirtha Swami of Śṛṅgerī Śāradā Pīṭha on 16 September 1985 during the celebration of the Silver Jubilee of *Śaṅkara Kripa,* a Telugu journal brought out under the auspices of the Pīṭha. Being the Vedāntic vision, it stands for what Murty stood and strived as a philosophy teacher. A pocket size book of 54 pages, it is divided into five sections as detailed below:

A. The Vedāntic teaching establishes that everyone's self is *Brahman.* The Vedic scriptures and the later commentators have spoken that the self is eternal, all-pervading, and the self of all and thus non-dual; and this Advaitic notion is possible through the study of the scriptures.

B. Both, Śaṅkara and the later Vedānta followers have asserted the falsity of the world, which lacks absolute reality and associated with *mithyā* (unknown).

C. Śaṅkara and his followers assert that the Upaniṣadic sentences are the means of valid knowledge for *brahma-jñāna.*

D. Scriptures are valid means for transcendental knowledge but not for empirical knowledge, though they refer to some points of history and science. Murty remarks that validity of the transcendental knowledge of Vedānta does not need any support from the modern scientific theories.

E. Murty proclaims that the metaphysical teachings of Advaita Vedānta implies, in the social sphere, equal-minded attitude and seeking the welfare of all beings, as Śaṅkarācārya comments that the true self is devoid of distinctions like *brāhmaṇa* and *kṣatriya.*

"Being" grounded in Hindu tradition, trained in Sanskrit language and learned in Vedāntic knowledge, Murty's commentary in the presence of the Śaṅkarācārya of Śṛṅgerī Śāradā Pīṭha about the social implications of Vedāntic metaphysics is noteworthy.

RADHAKRISHNAN: HIS LIFE AND IDEAS (1989)

This is a book for which Murty has collected for a long time the information and material relating to the life of Radhakrishnan, and utilized the literary talent of Ashok Vohra as co-author. Murty quotes, "It may be said of a philosopher or a scientist that 'the essential in the being' of such a man lies in what and how he thinks, not in what he does or suffers", which is what Einstein said about himself. Murty had produced this biography on the offer made by the Ministry of Information and Broadcasting, Government of India, in 1981.

This work on S. Radhakrishnan is divided into seventeen chapters, beginning from childhood to the august position, the President of India. Though based upon extensive research, it seems to be like a novel that creates enthusiasm in the reader. The life of Radhakrishnan starting from cities of Madras (Chennai) to Delhi through the cities of Rajahmundry, Mysore, Calcutta (Kolkata), Visakhapatnam and Benares has been described vividly. His life in England and Russia with political fibre has been depicted without intellectual gymnastics.

A real biography of a great philosopher came out through the hands of a real philosopher and a committed teacher of philosophy. It is useful to prescribe as a non-detailed text for graduate students, because of its lucid style, expository nature, authenticity of information, and classification of chapters.

VEDIC HERMENEUTICS (1993)

A masterpiece of interpretation by Murty on the Vedas, the book is divided into three chapters. The right approach to the study of Vedas maintained by the schools of Mīmāṁsā and Vedānta, and the qualifications and eligibility to the study of Veda are the content of the first chapter. On the basis of scriptural evidences, Murty argues for the eligibility of all Indians to study the Vedas, irrespective of sex, age and caste.

The second chapter enumerates how the contents of this sacred lore, Vedas can be interpreted through *tarka* (logic) and faith. The interpretative methodology adopted by various schools and scholars and the place of Vedas according to *Manusmṛti*, the *Mahābhārata*, the *Rāmāyaṇa* and the *Bhagavad-Gītā* are described.

The last chapter brings out the unity and essence of Vedas, in which the harmonization of Vedic sacrifices and knowledge is found. The spirit and goal of each part of the Veda — Saṁhitās, Brāhmaṇas, Āraṇyakas and Upaniṣads are noted. In every paragraph of this book Vedic words and their meaning, interpretation and application are found, which instil a new perspective on our knowledge of the Vedas.

1

The Vedas

Vedic Tradition

The Vedas are the earliest scriptures of ancient India. The word *veda* is a comprehensive one; it is this nature that led to various meanings made by different scholars. *Veda* means knowledge, feeling and an assertion. In the dictionaries, Veda is referred to the ancient sacred books of Hinduism, consisting of psalms, chants, etc. But it is universally acknowledged that the "*Veda* is a term applied to a group of literature that forms the earliest record of the Indian civilization"; and the primary meaning of the term *veda* is "a certain group of texts".[1]

The age of the Vedas is known as the Vedic period, usually dated approximately between 2500 and 6000 BC. This is the period in which the foundations of Indian culture were established, in which two fundamental aspects of Indian thought and life, the two paths of life — the active and the contemplative — were developed and formulated in the Vedas and Upaniṣads, respectively.

The Vedas have been the most sacred texts for Hindus in the annals of Indian history. It is believed that men never composed the Vedas; they were either taught by God to the sages or revealed to the sages who were the seers of the hymns (*mantra-draṣṭā*). The practices mentioned in the Vedic literature are being practised even today. The Hindu community, at the

[1] C. Kunhan Raja, *Vedas*, p. 1.

time of birth and death, performs the rituals according to the old tradition; they are being performed to propitiate the deities, as described in the ancient Vedic literature. Some members of the brāhmaṇa community, even nowadays, offer prayers three times a day, which were used as prayers 3,000 years ago as per the Vedic sacrifices and rituals.

The Vedas consist of passages mostly in the form of prayers addressed to a large number of deities; they are aerial, earthly and heavenly gods, worshipped in different forms. The poems, which are usually designated as hymns are called in Sanskrit the *sūkta*s (or what has been well spoken).[2] Yāska has written a dictionary to the Vedas, which is called *Nirukta.* It is explained that the eternal Veda manifested itself in the minds of persons performing *tapas* (penance);[3] but it has been believed that Veda is not a product of humans *apauruṣeya.* The Vedas indicate human feelings and aspirations, and contain a kind of notation. The Veda is said to be divine, applicable to the past, present and future; it is religious, eternal and meditative.

MURTY'S COMMENTARY

The Vedas were not found in one place in India, but spread over to many regions in the country. Both in the north and south, especially in some places of Andhra Pradesh, Karnataka, Maharashtra, Gujarat, Uttar Pradesh, Bihar and Odisha, a number of brāhmaṇa families by-hearted the Vedas and transmitted it to the later generations. Murty says that it is very difficult for a person to by-heart any meagre portion of the Vedas or not possible for a family even. The four Vedas have been kept recited in various places by different brāhmaṇa families, which resulted in recitation of a particular thought of the Veda by a particular family. A family of a particular

[2] C. Kunhan Raja, *Vedas,* p. 2.

[3] K. Satchidananda Murty, *Vedic Hermeneutics,* p. 5.

region was not aware of the other part of the Vedas recited by other different families in another region.

Since ancient times, the Vedas have been by-hearted by brāhmaṇa families, but no attempt was made to understand the etymological meaning of the Veda. Therefore Yāska made an attempt to furnish the meaning of the unknown and rare words that occur in the Vedas, and wrote the *Nirukta.* Hence to comprehend the meaning of Vedic words, syllables and *mantras*, it is necessary to consult the *Nirukta* of Yāska. He is of the opinion that a number of *mantra*s in the Vedas are intelligible and contradictory; yet one should not find fault with them, probably the ignorance of their meaning is due to our inability. However on the basis of the commentary written by Sāyaṇa in the fourteenth century CE, the Vedas have been translated and published.

In pursuance of the study of the Vedas, Murty says that the modern man, who is aware of the origin and development of the language and science, does not accept any book whether it is the Veda or the Quran or any other sacred book as eternal and composed by God.[4] However, Murty asserts that, in accordance with the tradition, the Veda is an eternal and infallible source of *dharma* (righteous action); it contains some of the perennial values, which have been apprehended by sages and prophets in ancient times, whether written in or revealed by God or discovered by man. It must be admitted that their assertions are relevant as far as they are connected with the unknowable truths, though contradicted by human experience and science.

Though Śaṅkara gave prominence to the texts of the Śruti or the Vedas and Vedānta, their relevance to the empirical fact was denied. It means if the Śruti text says that fire is cold,

[4] K. Satchidananda Murty, *Vedic Hermeneutics*, p. 5.

it should not be believed so. With reference to the empirical aspect, the knowledge of the scriptures is not applicable. Similarly Murty rejects some assertions of the scientists for their fusion of scientific proofs with religious doctrines. Murty says that the standpoint of Śaṅkara, which bifurcates the empirical knowledge and the divine knowledge, is right.

Murty also remarks that no scripture is unique whether it is revealed or discovered, as it has to be recorded and communicated by human intellect. In other words due to the involvement of human intellect even the infinite knowledge will also become finite. Further, Murty does not accept that the divine knowledge is revealed to a particular race. It is no doubt that some of the scriptures contain some sort of historical and scientific ideas which may be, sometimes, helpful for the reconstruction of the social and political history of the people or nation. But one has to remember that the ideas relating to the historical and scientific nature do not form the core of the scripture.

In accordance with his standpoint that one need not draw scientific support for the theological questions, Murty remarks in his *Vedic Hermeneutics* that the Vedic tradition "avoids all possible conflicts between scriptures on the one hand and history and science on the other."[5] Śaṅkarācārya has also said that if the Veda says that fire is cold and opposes the empirical facts, one need not believe the Vedic sentences. In this context Murty says that the historical facts and scientific truths would not be opposed by scriptural assertions. While critically examining the texts, Murty is of the opinion that though the Vedas are sacred and revealed records of ancient seers, but their assertions on empirical facts need not be accepted, if differ from concrete realities. It is in accordance with the Vācaspati assertion in *Bhāmati;* he writes:

---

[5] K. Satchidananda Murty, *Vedic Hermeneutics*, p. 4.

> As Vācaspati observes in *Bhāmati,* the Vedas are not valued just because they are tradition. Only when they have the strength of perception and support of logic, are they to be esteemed: *tātparyavatī śruti, pratyakṣad balavatī, na śruti mātram.* The Vedas are, no doubt, the recordings of the experiments in the science of spirit by our forefathers. They have much truth in them. But associated with it, there are also found recorded some of their beliefs and views on other matters also, which appear ridiculous at the present day. But this is inevitable. Nowhere can we procure the grain without the husk, the egg without its shell and the rose without its thorns.[6]

Similar to the acceptance of changes in science, Murty says that we should also accept changes in theology. He reminds us of the ancient scholarly discussion about the Vedas. He says *anantaḥ vai vedaḥ,* "endless are the Vedas". The Veda has not ceased to develop. It has neither an end nor a beginning.[7] In other words Vedas contain experiences of the seers, their beliefs, views and certain truths; but the validity of them depends upon the strength it derives from perception and logic. Murty writes:

> Spiritual perception is no exception to the laws of logic, spiritual experiences, when interpreted in a right and intelligent manner, should not go contra to the nature and laws of our everyday world.[8]

About the Vedic recitation, Murty draws our attention to the importance of knowing the verbal meaning of the Vedas. Chanting the verses in an appropriate manner and reciting symphonically is a meritorious thing; this practice has also been there in many cultures and religions. Murty also observed

[6] K. Satchidananda Murty, *Hinduism and Its Development,* p. 18.

[7] Ibid., p. 20.

[8] Ibid., p. 18.

that, in the contemporary times, many are chanting without knowing its meaning and some are doing without understanding. On perusal it is observed that neither of them has firm faith in the intrinsic power of the Vedic words. Therefore, Murty remarks that this state of affairs should be transformed. He reminds us that the Veda says that one does not really hear the Veda if one does it without knowing its meaning. A person who learns Veda without knowing the meaning is like a pillar that carries the load of a house. For him the sacrifices performed in a mechanical way and Vedic sentence repeated in a parrot-like fashion are not completely efficacious. Here Murty's comments are worth noting:

> If today the teaching of Veda is not as widely known as the teachings of the Bible, the Quran, the *Bhagavad-Gītā* and some other scriptures are, it is because it has not been disseminated among the general public.[9]

The efforts made by certain individuals like Swami Dayananda Saraswati and institutions have yielded little results. In this direction the five significant portions of the Vedas should be selected, translated and reinterpreted in a way appealing to the modern mind. Similar to the *Bhagavad-Gītā* and the Upaniṣads, the important Vedic portions and the popular scriptures should be made available to the public. For centuries Vedic study was limited to the three upper castes, especially the brāhmaṇas. It should be taught to everybody as per the *Yajurveda,* which asserts as follows:

> Just as I have revealed this auspicious word to all human beings, so must you. I have revealed the Vedic truth to brāhmaṇas, kṣatriyas, śūdras, Āryans, personal servants (*svaya*) and to the lowest of śūdras (*araṇaya*) also.[10]

---

[9] K. Satchidananda Murty, *Vedic Hermeneutics,* pp. 8-9.

[10] Ibid., p. 14.

Murty asserts that the Veda is a universal scripture, for the children of the slaves and śūdras have been the authors of the some of the *mantras* of the *Ṛgveda.* For example, Mahidāsa Ātreya was the son of a brāhmaṇa sage and a low caste woman, Itara. He became a great sage and authored the *Aitareya Brāhmaṇa,* and *Āraṇyaka.* In the Upaniṣads it is recorded that Janaśruti who was called the śūdra and Satyakāma Jābāli, who was the son of a maid servant and whose father is not known, have been considered as the men of highest Vedāntic knowledge. Lopāmudrā and Apālā were the two women mentioned as the authors of some *mantras* of the *Ṛgveda;* Gārgī and Maitreyī were the two ladies considered as the women who possessed the highest Upaniṣadic truth.

Regarding the right to study the Vedas by śūdras, women and others, there are negative and positive statements in the Smṛtis. Murty says that the Veda is a universal scripture meant for all human beings and everybody should be allowed to study the Vedas. He concludes:

> Good sense, justice and reason demand that the latter view be accepted. Everyone has the right to the highest wisdom from the best source available. Moreover, as the Western scholars (who according to some Smṛti writers would be *mlecchas*) as well as those who are not of three castes, *traivarṇikas* (e.g. Prince Dara Shikoh, Swami Vivekananda and Sri Aurobindo) have studied, edited, translated, expounded, or published the Vedas and Upaniṣads, it is not only unjust and ridiculous to support anymore the taboo on Vedic study. People of all castes including the "Harijans" and "Girijans" and of all nationalities — irrespective of their sex — should be encouraged to study the Veda.[11]

---

[11] K. Satchidananda Murty, *Vedic Hermeneutics,* p. 17.

THE VEDIC STUDY

The Vedas have influenced Indians for centuries. To comprehend their significance they have to be taken as a whole on the one hand, and should be studied according to the traditional pattern taking into consideration their meaning and purport (*tātparya*) on the other hand. Murty clarifies that the Western Indologists studied the Vedas believing that they are the collections of the primitive people and tried to fix the date on the basis of the language and the ideas in them, which is nothing but the method based upon comparative philology and methodology. They did not study the Vedas in the way in which for thousands of years it was studied as a Holy Scriptures in India. Therefore Murty, similar to Karl Geidner and Richard Pischel, says that the Vedas should be studied taking into consideration the historical context, the later literature and the indigenous tradition. In other words the Vedas should be understood and interpreted through the "study of all spheres of Indian life and literature, familiar with Indian thinking and feeling".[12]

The Veda is interpreted in many ways as it has many meanings. In ancient times a number of sages have written many commentaries, similarly competent and qualified persons are free to interpret the Veda. Murty writes that the different schools of Mīmāṁsā and Vedānta have discussed the way in which the meaning of the Vedas is to be ascertained. He remarks:

> Both Mīmāṁsā and Vedānta are hermeneutic philosophies, in which exegesis, apologetics, epistemology, metaphysics and ethics are synthesized. Mīmāṁsā is primarily concerned with duty and/or righteousness and Vedānta with the knowledge of ultimate reality.[13]

---

[12] K. Satchidananda Murty, *Vedic Hermeneutics*, p. 27.

[13] Ibid., p. 32.

The classification of the Vedas into two different portions — portions dealing with action (*karma-kāṇḍa*) and portions dealing with knowledge (*jñāna-kāṇḍa*) — has to be reconciled while understanding the Vedas. It is no doubt the earlier portions of the Vedas contain hymns in praise of gods and description of rituals, and the later portions centred on the ultimate reality in the form of dialogues. But the greatest interpreter of the Vedas, Sāyaṇa asserted the unity of meaning and purport of all the Vedas as follows:

> Through all the Vedas it is, indeed, *Brahman* that is ascertained. This is well known in the case of their Upaniṣadic portions; even in the case of their other portions, which have sacrifice, etc., as their subject, as through purification of mind they become the means of knowing *Brahman*. The later (i.e. *Brahman*) becomes their subject.[14]

Therefore, though there is difference between the earlier and later portions of Vedas, there is mutual coherence. This has been the traditional understanding put forward by Sāyaṇa, Śaṅkarācārya and other Vedānta teachers. Even the modern Western scholars Maurice, Bloomfield and Louis Renou have accepted the fact that there is no opposition in the earlier and later portions of the Vedas.

Murty observes that the Vedāntic teaching is nothing but what is in accordance with the Upaniṣadic message; for which the supreme goal in this world is nothing but the realization of the unity of the individual self with the Supreme Self.[15] This is the self-knowledge that results in one's own experience; thus it cannot be spoken as it is self-evident and self-proved. The unity of self is established on the strength of awareness.

---

[14] *Sāyaṇa Bhāṣya* on the *Ṛgveda* 1.164-39; cited from K. Satchidananda Murty, *Vedic Hermeneutics*, p. 76.

[15] K. Satchidananda Murty, *The Advaitic Notion*, p. 10.

According to later Advaita Vedānta though the world is indefinable it is unspeakable.[16] Murty writes: "If one has no conception of Advaita, a proof of it cannot be asked."[17] The self-knowledge arises out of Vedāntic sentences; such knowledge is the self-luminous and eternal, which gives liberation. He concludes: "Self-awareness which is self-proved is undeniable and ineffable. This is *vijñāna* or *Brahman*."[18] He also writes, in accordance with Advaitic tradition that the falsity of the world is spoken in order to help one to experience non-duality; finally he clarifies that according to Advaita Vedānta "neither the world nor its falsity are absolutely real".[19]

The knowledge of *Brahman* according to Śaṅkara derives from the Upaniṣadic sentences only; the other *pramāṇa*s (means of knowledge) may be accepted only if they support Upaniṣadic thinking. The great sentences (*mahāvākya*s) of the Upaniṣads represent the summary of the essence of Vedānta literature, and help one to obtain direct, immediate awareness (*sākṣātkāra*) of *Brahman*. Here Murty upholds a new interpretation:

> If an ethical person with a pure and subtle mind who has gone through the Vedāntic discipline is convinced that he has it, he must be right. The testimony for *Brahman*-knowing is the feeling within one's own heart.[20]

Murty perceived the scriptural knowledge with special reference to the social facts and aspects, in the beginning of his academic career and as well as dialectically interpreted them in his later writings. He has critically interpreted even

[16] K. Satchidananda Murty, *The Advaitic Notion*, p. 10.

[17] Ibid., p. 11.

[18] Ibid., p. 17.

[19] Ibid., p. 23.

[20] Ibid., pp. 27-28.

the Vedic doctrines and assertions. In accordance with the *Bhagavad-Gītā*'s assertions that he who has the equal-mind will engage in the welfare of all beings, Murty says: "the ethical and socio-political implications of Advaita Vedānta are also important."[21]

He remarks that vision and practice should not be different; one should not have a split personality; *Advaita* and *samatva* in thought and deed should go together. Murty refers to the ethical value propounded by Hastāmalaka, a disciple of Śaṅkara, who echoed the indivisible oneness of all.[22] The root of this fruitful interpretation could also be found in the Śaṅkara's commentary on the *Bṛhadāraṇyaka Upaniṣad,* which says that "the true self is devoid of distinctions like brāhmaṇa, kṣatriya, etc.; caste, life-stage, age, situation, etc., are superimposed on it".[23] Murty argues that a man who realizes that the same self lives in all human beings does not harm either himself or the other. Finally he concludes the spirit of Vedānta as follows:

> The consequence of the awareness of Identity necessarily results in equality. The metaphysics of Advaita can be the foundation only for unselfishness and altruism and is consistent only with an egalitarian society based on social and economic justice, equality and peace.[24]

The Upaniṣads contain the search for infinite power that controls and sustains the world. They are, for Murty, like gem or diamond that glitters and scatters its shining rays, though one is not able to understand what diamond is, yet claims the perception of a diamond. Similarly truth is one and

[21] K. Satchidananda Murty, *The Advaitic Notion,* p. 42.

[22] Ibid., p. 54.

[23] Ibid., p. 51.

[24] Ibid., p. 43.

people speak of it divergently; God is one but the wise people call it with different names, *ekaṁ sat viprāḥ bahudhā vadanti.* In this context Murty says that "thought gives us only imperfect and distorted pictures of reality"; and "reality is neither an idea nor a conception"; it is beyond thought, only intuition can grasp it. Intuitive knowledge cannot be grasped with intellectual perception.[25]

Murty affirms that reality is the absolute and cannot be grasped with empirical and mundane methods; neither genius nor much learning helps one to reach the core of reality. All thoughts and desires and intellectual exercises should be stopped to attain the real knowledge of the absolute reality, which is the result of the disciplined meditation. Truth is known, when the mental faculties are controlled. It is to be remembered that intellect and reason have their own domain but cannot help to know the absolute reality. Logic and reason — the faculties of intellect — are related to the empirical world or the phenomenal world; but the noumenon is the domain of absolute reality, which could be known through intuition.

The Absolute Reality spoken in the Upaniṣads is *Brahman,* which is the source, provider and the end of everything. The power of *Brahman,* it is said, is to manifest itself in the activities of the mind. *Brahman* is the fundamental substratum of the universe, and the unmanifested supreme power. In a dialogue between Śvetaketu and his father, Uddālaka Āruṇi, *Brahman* is spoken as that which underlies everything in the universe and also in one self. It implies the oneness of the life of the man and that of the universe. In this context Murty interprets that human experience in the physical world and nature leads to adoration of nature and the worship of things in it; thus originated various gods, and in course of time evolves a supreme God among different gods, i.e. *Brahman.* Murty

[25] K. Satchidananda Murty, *Hinduism and Its Development,* p. 13.

interprets that Hinduism is one of the established religions of the world and predominant in India. Because of the diverse doctrines absorbed into it during its long evolution, and because of the latitude, allowed in the interpretation of its scriptures, there have been many systems and beliefs, which can be said to represent Hinduism.[26]

The belief in the eternity of the soul or self (*puruṣa, ātman*) is nearly universal among Hindus. What is living and vital in Indian philosophy today is the Vedānta system in its various forms, it is the living religion of the Hindus and is the clear native philosophy of India, whose popular name is Hinduism.

It is well-known that Hindu religion grew out of Vedic thought primarily, the second part of the Vedas is called the third part of Āraṇyakas and the ending or the fourth part of the Vedas is called the Upaniṣads, which are considered to be primary sources for the Vedāntic thinking. Śaṅkara teaches that liberation should be the highest aim of man; and that it can be achieved through renunciation of action through the inward realization of one's identity with the Supreme Spirit (*Brahman*). He believed that right action and sacrifice are only instruments to purify the mind, but did not give liberation. Keeping in the spirit of the Vedāntic scriptures, Murty asserts:

> People, who worship different gods, people who worship the same god in different ways, people worship no god at all can all be Hindus.[27]

According to Śaṅkara, the Vedic scriptures are meant for acquiring the religious duties, whereas Vedāntic teachings culminated in personal experience and result in the knowledge of *Brahman*. Religious actions are related to human efforts; the Vedic texts prescribe the rules and methodology of their

---

[26] Paul Edwards (ed.), *The Encyclopaedia of Philosophy*, vol. IV, p. 1.

[27] K. Satchidananda Murty, *Hinduism and Its Development*, p. 16.

performance. Actions may be performed or may not be performed or can be done in different ways like a man, who wants to go somewhere or to Gandhāra region can go on foot or by horse or by cart. Thus one's choice depends on one's notions. In this context, Murty remarks:

> Religion, according to the Hindus, is neither the celebration of ceremonies nor the acceptance of a set of irrational beliefs.[28]

For Murty religion is not intended to alienate man from the real world. It means if religion does not have any practical views, people might have left it long back. It is not intended to make us to adopt superstitious silliness and orthodox foolishness, but religion meant to serve practical ends, to help him and to grow himself in the society with a living history. He writes:

> The role of religion does not stop with showing men what they are; it also shows them how to shape the course of life in the light of what they are.[29]

Murty believes that "the value of religion lies in the practical direction it gives to day-to-day life".[30] Religion makes man to understand the inner truth of all existence. Religion never tolerates either the egoistic veiling or the emotional distortions. Religion provides hope and security for smooth sailing of human life; a mundane life becomes joyful, richer and full when man becomes spiritual. He says that the *Ṛta,* spoken in the *Ṛgveda,* is the law immanent in all beings, it is the higher law; it is the inner law of the spirit that differs from man-made laws. If one is spiritual and has the divine glow, he himself becomes the law. Such a man need not look

---

[28] K. Satchidananda Murty, *Hinduism and Its Development*, p. 17.

[29] Ibid., p. 55.

[30] Ibid., p. 60.

into the outer world, external authority and commandments. This kind of interpretation of Murty is close to Kant's concept of "Categorical Imperative" and the Vedāntic notion of sainthood or *jīvan-mukta*. He writes:

> When thus once the soul attains the real and eternal . . . all that is mean will simply be burnt up. . . . His will become God's will and God's will become his. Those who have achieved this cannot do anything evil. The saint's activity will spontaneously be saintly. If the striving and sincerity are there, the possibility of becoming one with the divine, God, is not a remote one. It can be realized here and now.[31]

Murty says that, the religious education integrates the spiritual and material aspects. Man is not simply either a brain or body but also a spirit. The head and heart should be kept together. Therefore there is a need for religious education. International co-operation, peace, human brotherhood and universal understanding come through the implementation of all-round education, which is possible through the awareness of the unity of all.

---

[31] K. Satchidananda Murty, *Hinduism and Its Development*, pp. 62-63.

2

Indian Philosophy

PROF. Murty says that the development of any kind of knowledge associated with human understanding depends upon social conditions and physical environment.[1] In his *Evolution of Philosophy in India*, Murty has interpreted Indian philosophy from the standpoint of socio-political and physical conditions at various periods of Indian history, which is an attempt close to Bertrand Russell's *A History of Western Philosophy*.

Murty held the view that neither a thinker nor a philosophy arose out of anything, for they being the product of their social and political institution.[2] He remarks that the study of the history of philosophy should not be governed by sentimental feelings, and at the same time the reader of Indian philosophy should be aware of the difference between religion and philosophy. In this context Murty asserts:

> Critics governed more by sentiment and feeling than by reason and truth may object to some passages in this book, while those who have not got over the confusion of philosophy with religion and are in the clutches of the belief that Indian thought is the best that has been ever produced and will be produced will be shocked by the views expressed herein. While none

---

[1] K. Satchidananda Murty, *Evolution of Philosophy in India*, Preface, p. i. (A revised version appeared as, *Evolution of Indian Philosophy*, in 2007.)

[2] Ibid., p. 2.

> can have greater regard and love for Indian culture and the Indian way of life than myself, I am for viewing things objectively and scientifically, unclogged by misplaced patriotism and love for the past. It is not popular opinion and patriotism that should guide one in assessing value of philosophical system.[3]

Written in his *Evolution of Philosophy in India,* a work of earlier days when he was young, this paragraph implies the following points, to be kept in mind while reading and interpreting Indian philosophy:

1. Every thinker and philosopher is the product of his or her social conditions and physical environment.
2. The distinction between religion and philosophy should be perceived clearly.
3. While understanding Indian philosophy, one should not be led away by sentiments and feelings but cultivate the rational mode of search for truth.
4. One should view things objectively and scientifically, unclogged by misplaced patriotism and love for the past.
5. While understanding the ideals and doctrines, there is a need to examine their roots in the society.

The emergence of Marxism has revolutionized human thought in understanding a society. Murty remembers how Marx has proposed that ideas and human thought reflect not only the socio-economic conditions but also have the necessary potentiality to break the established social and political institutions, causing to raise new social factors and conditions. Thus ideas make history and also some of the ideas, which do not fit into the existing social structure, will fail to be effective.

[3] K. Satchidananda Murty, *Evolution of Philosophy in India,* Preface, p. i.

Murty says, even the ideas of God and the nature of God, described in different religions are due to the social and physical conditions of the regions, where they arose.[4] In this context Murty also brings out the contradictory point involved in deriving conclusions. For him, though ideas have their roots in social conditions their value cannot be judged on the basis of the prevailing conditions. For example, the Christian conception of the "end of the world" was the result of the simple thinking of the Galilean peasantry, amidst the Roman Empire, where nobody believed that the world comes to an end. Similarly the golden maxim of Christ "Love thy neighbour as thyself" cannot be verified by an observation of facts, whether it is a wish or command.

With reference to the evolution of Indian philosophy Murty comments that the six schools of Indian philosophy are due to the influence of socio-economic conditions of north India, which caused the development of the pessimistic view of life, seeking salvation to get away from this world.[5] But Murty points out that the majority of the people neither worked out for their salvation nor tried to escape from the world as desired by the spiritual interpreters of Indian philosophy. Therefore he asserts that all intellectual activities including religion and ethics are associated both with conscious and unconscious instinct of the mind. The instincts of man are the prime movers of all human activity, says Murty. Similarly one's own education also influences one's perspective and thinking process. The point to be noted here is that the psychology of the person will also play a vital role in moulding one's philosophical thought. He writes:

> Thus the study of a man's character, of his habits and environment provides a clue towards understanding and

[4] K. Satchidananda Murty, *Evolution of Philosophy in India,* p. 3.

[5] Ibid., p. 6.

> appreciating his theories and beliefs. Not only is it necessary to study any theory in relation to the socio-economic structure in which it arises, but it is also necessary to pay attention to the character and personality of the man who puts it forth.[6]

The formation of Indian thought, according to Murty, has its roots in the fusion of races in ancient India. The anthropologists confirmed that the Indian population consists of all sorts of races — black, white and yellow. These ethnic races that arrived to India in ancient times must be the cause for the rise of caste system, which certainly resulted in different racial memories and thoughts; he observes:

> These different races with their different racial memories and thoughts must have looked upon each other with suspicion and contempt. The Āryans were the conquerors. But the conquered were highly superior to them in culture and social organization. Both had points of which they could be proud. The different original races and the cross-breeds with their endless variety of customs, creed and social environment must have gone on living for some time. Then a sort of common culture must have resulted. But it was never a homogeneous and uniform culture. This is illustrated by the Vedic and Upaniṣadic literature.[7]

The different doctrines claimed by the brāhmaṇas and the kṣatriyas, found in the Upaniṣads reflect the claims of different castes over the metaphysical knowledge and rigidity of caste system. Because of the invasion and arrival of different races different social environment developed, which resulted in plurality of doctrines and thoughts in Indian thought. Murty emphasizes, this fact for understanding Indian philosophy:

---

[6] K. Satchidananda Murty, *Evolution of Philosophy in India,* p. 13.

[7] Ibid., p. 31.

> This is an objective fact which ought to be recognized as such. There is no use of getting emotional and saying as some Indians do that all this is false and that Indian thought is the best, the noblest, the most logical and the most spiritual in the world.[8]

ON THE HISTORY OF INDIAN PHILOSOPHY

Murty observed that the writers of the histories of Indian philosophy have simply narrated each system without evaluating and examining the facts with figures. The other defect in the histories of philosophy is that they confuse religion with philosophy, though these two are not identical.[9] A number of Indian traditional interpreters and Western modern writers of Indian philosophy — especially Max Müller, Paul Deussen and Richard Garbe have identified that certain sections and portions of Indian philosophy are not philosophical at all. Max Müller has remarked that the word *darśana* cannot be translated as philosophy.[10]

Therefore Murty says that while writing history of Indian philosophy the distinction between philosophy and theology should be maintained; and the difference between the systematic thought and belief should be kept in mind.[11]

A number of parallel thoughts or striking similarities are found between thinkers of India and philosophers of the West. Comparisons have been made between Śaṅkara's Advaita and portions of St. John of the Cross. The conception of history found in *Śrīmad Bhāgavatam* and the Bible seems to be similar; studies have been undertaken comparing Śaṅkara and Bradley.

---

[8] K. Satchidananda Murty, *Evolution of Philosophy in India,* pp. 33-34.

[9] Ibid., pp. 41-42.

[10] Ibid., p. 42.

[11] Ibid., p. 44.

According to Murty comparison does not make any school logical; but the validity of any system depends upon the consistency of its own doctrines. If at all any comparison is to be made with reference to Indian philosophy, it can be compared to the Medieval Scholasticism only. He writes:

> My point for the present is that scholastic philosophy and Indian philosophy resemble each other to a great deal, while there is no resemblance between Indian philosophy and modern philosophy of the West.[12]

Both scholasticism and Indian philosophy are similar and aimed to systematize and rationalize religious dogmas. The scholastic thinkers did not care to acquaint themselves with the development of geography and physical sciences made by the Greeks and Arabs. Similarly in India too, the philosophers never considered the work of the materialists, Cārvākas and the medical man, Suśruta; but went on describing their conception of soul and allied problems, when the Indians travelled to the Far East countries like Java, Sumatra, Cambodia and many other places. Śaṅkara, Rāmānuja and other Vedāntins go on discussing about the souls' travels to the moon, and believed in the existence of seven *lokas* (heavenly abodes) above and the seven below, and about the ocean of milk and honey, the Meru mountain, etc.[13] Contrary to the scientific discoveries made by the Indian astronomers, the Indian religious texts contained sentences about cosmology that are far away from truth.

Finally Murty says that there are certain systematic schools like the Sāṁkhya, which adhered to reason. Though there have been splendid efforts to analyse and articulate questions and discussions regarding the issues they have taken up, all those

---

[12] K. Satchidananda Murty, *Evolution of Philosophy in India*, p. 46.

[13] Ibid., p. 47.

laborious learnings proceeded on the basis of the scriptures they believe or the master they worship. Though a clear distinction between philosophy and theology, reason and faith did not find in the systems of Indian philosophy, there is a need and possibility to extract philosophy from the mythological and historical writings of India. Murty asserts:

> We do not find any clear distinction between philosophy and theology, reason and faith as is found in Thomas Aquinas. On the other hand, there are systems like classical Sāṁkhya, which though they rely on tradition (*āpta-vacana*) are atheistic. In the case of all the schools it is possible to some extent to extract their philosophy from their concomitant theological and mythological trappings, and assess the value of such philosophy. But Pūrva-Mīmāṁsā and Yoga must be put aside while we are concerned with philosophy. Only then can a history of Indian philosophy be accomplished, which it can be asserted is no light task.[14]

INTERPRETATION OF INDIAN PHILOSOPHY

Murty was influenced, it seems, by Bertrand Russell. He started interpreting Indian philosophy in the context of social, political and economic background, in his *Hinduism and Its Development* at the age of twenty-three. In his interpretation, one could find geographical and physical conditions as causes for the origin of Hinduism, apart from the racial differences. According to him, probably the influence of Islam in Kerala, might have caused Śaṅkara to undertake adventurous journey, through hills and forests with fervour and faith, to defend the religion of the Hindus through his interpretation of Vedānta.[15] Murty also stated the influence of Islam on the thought of Kabīr and Nānak, and the socio-political and

[14] K. Satchidananda Murty, *Evolution of Philosophy in India*, p. 51.

[15] K. Satchidananda Murty, *Hinduism and Its Development*, p. 117.

educational reforms of the British in India for the rise of new outlook in Hinduism.[16] In his *Evolution of Philosophy in India* he traced the social and political conditions for the formation of Indian mind.

He proclaims that he wanted to present Indian philosophy objectively and scientifically. According to him all the heterodox schools are the results of speculative outlook of sixth century BC at which time the authority of the priests and the validity of magical cults, the worship of God and goddesses have been questioned.[17]

The Buddha, being the son of a kṣatriya ruler from the pedigree of Śākyas, has been the critic of brāhmaṇas, according to whom the true brāhmaṇa is one who is virtuous and learned, but not he who is born in the brāhmaṇa caste.[18] Buddha's criticism of the brāhmaṇas at various occasions, according to Murty, shows the social background and also reflects the modern concept of class outlook while professing views and comments. This implies, Murty opines:

> Every ideology — political, philosophical or religious — arises in answer to a particular problem of a particular age and part of the country.[19]

Apart from his earlier works, Murty also argued in his later works that social, political and economic institutions shape the views and theories, though man is a free and creative being and yet being influenced by socio-political and geographical conditions. He cited the Marxist view in support of his assertions as:

---

[16] K. Satchidananda Murty, *Hinduism and Its Development*, p. 132.

[17] K. Satchidananda Murty, *Evolution of Philosophy in India*, p. 105.

[18] Ibid., p. 106.

[19] Ibid., p. 149.

> Philosophers do not grow out of the soil like mushrooms; they are the product of their time and of their people.[20]

In this context Murty says that philosophy can be understood better, if the political, social and economic circumstances are studied. In accordance with the interpretation of the American philosopher, William James, Murty asserts that the individual situation in life and experiences also, to some extent, penetrate into the process of human thinking. Though the situations are similar, yet each individual perceives things differently; no two individuals, who have come from the same background, need to have the same point of view or the same way of thinking. Sometimes not only thinking differs from each other, but certain people think further ahead of others. Therefore the evolution of ideas, the growth of thinking can be better understood only when the beliefs, attitudes, expectations and social structure are better studied. In the same society and at the same time each class has its own way of looking at things and interpreting the same in a different way. Murty writes:

> But no society is entirely homogeneous; for every society there are various strata, and conflicting interests and impulses, and so different ways of looking at things and interpretation-experience and building up knowledge. Not only different cultures, ages and societies have different perspectives, but the different strata in the same society have different perspectives, all of which mutually influence each other and some of which may at times merge into each other.[21]

ĀṆVIKṢIKĪ AS INDIAN PHILOSOPHY

Murty, while explaining philosophy in India not only discussed about *darśana* but also recorded the different words that were

[20] Marx and Engels, *On Religion*, Cf. K. Satchidananda Murty, *Indian Philosophy Since 1498*, p. 21.

[21] Ibid., p. 22.

used in Sanskrit literature. *Brahmodaya* is the word that is used to denote philosophical or theological discussions in the Vedic literature. In the later Vedic literature the same speculative discussions have been denoted by the words *ātma-vidyā, parā-vidyā.* The Buddhists used the *dṛṣṭi* or *ditthi* to denote the philosophical viewpoint; similarly the *Bhagavad-Gītā* refers philosophy as *tattva-jñāna.* But Murty prefers *āṇvikṣikī* as an appropriate word to denote philosophy. Kauṭilya, in his *Arthaśāstra,* classified knowledge into four kinds; in which *āṇvikṣikī* is stated to be the "science of review" which differs from the other three — the Vedic study (theology), economics (agriculture) and politics. Here Murty summarizes what *āṇvikṣikī* is:

> *Āṇvikṣikī,* according to Kauṭilya, reviews (examines) with the help of arguments, the contents of the other three sciences and their strengths and weaknesses, makes reason steadfast and balanced in adversity and prosperity, and clarifies one's insight, speech and action. It, he continues, is the lamp of all sciences, the aid to all actions, and the basis of all virtues.[22]

Murty writes that according to Kauṭilya the systems of Indian thought — the Sāṁkhya, Vaiśeṣika and the Lokāyata schools — constitute *āṇvikṣikī.* Subsequently in the later works *āṇvikṣikī* is used to denote as the "science of self" (*ātma-vidya*) and the "science of reasoning" (*nyāya*). Though in the ancient times, philosophy was conceived as *āṇvikṣikī,* which helps to analyse the potentiality of one's behaviour, unfortunately over the centuries this conception receded due to the domination of the *darśana* concept of philosophy as essentially ontology and metaphysics conducive to liberation.[23]

---

[22] K. Satchidananda Murty, *Philosophy in India,* p. 5.

[23] Ibid., p. 173.

FUTURE OF PHILOSOPHY

Murty analyses the lacuna in the philosophical thinking of philosophy teachers in India. He writes that for some scholars any kind of religious, ethical and political thinking seems to be the soft philosophy. For others only analytical, logical schools of the West are the right proto-type of philosophy. Murty emphasizes that it would be a mistake to consider only metaphysics, epistemology and logic as the whole of philosophy.[24] He also remarks that, apart from this kind of perception, the contributions of the philosophers on human welfare and progress have also been considered as philosophy.

There has been a uniform opinion about Western philosophy in Indian universities, but not on the ancient Indian philosophy or contemporary philosophy. Though M.N. Roy and Jiddu Krishnamurti were far superior in their analysis of Indian philosophy and thought, the philosophy teachers in the universities have not considered them as philosophers; however they have great following in the country. If philosophy is considered as discussion and analysis of all ideas and ideologies relating to poetic, scientific, religious, legal, political, social and educational aspects, automatically the studies of our ancient, medieval and modern writers on law, sociology, history and politics will also be considered as philosophies.

The inconsistency in the philosophical understanding of contemporary thinkers has been analysed by Murty. He comments that some critics consider Vivekananda, Ramana Maharshi and Gandhi as philosophers and neglect the philosophy of Narayana Guru, Chandrasekhar Bharati and Ambedkar. Murty opined that initiative has to be taken in the case of Vinoba Bhave and Jayaprakash Narayan and Ambedkar at large.

---

[24] K. Satchidananda Murty, *Philosophy in India,* p. 179.

As early as in 1966 the University Grants Commission (UGC) published a report, *Philosophy in Indian Universities.* The report suggests that there must be a critical evaluation of Indian philosophy and also there should be an infusion of Western and Indian philosophies; and the issues of our times should be studied including the modern schools of Indian philosophy.[25]

In *Philosophy in India,* Murty also reviewed the discussions published by the UGC in 1978 related to the four workshops — Philosophy Teaching in India: New Perspectives and Programmes — organized in 1975-76 at four places in Indian universities. The report of 1978 advocates to teach and emphasize on the relevance of philosophy in everyday life, giving the following conclusions:

1. The rich and varied philosophical heritage of India should be taught with social relevance.
2. What is not relevant in the traditional Indian philosophy should be discarded; and what is universal and best for now is to be taught.
3. With critical outlook, various ideologies and systems of Western and Indian should be taught to arrive and develop an adequate value system.
4. Various philosophical problems as perceived and answered by each philosopher should be taught.[26]

The report suggests that though metaphysics and epistemology are the core of philosophy, a greater emphasis is needed on moral and political philosophies, philosophy of education, philosophy of religion, etc. In this context, Murty says that there should not be any uniform curriculum

---

[25] K. Satchidananda Murty, *Philosophy in India,* p. 165.

[26] Ibid., p. 167.

throughout the country, providing autonomy to the universities and philosophy teachers.

> I think it is good that universities should be entirely autonomous, provided they have internal democratization; and this implies that every university department should be free to conduct its affairs in its own way with all its teachers equally participating in every one of its decisions and activities.[27]

India has a long, rich, continuous and most varied philosophical heritage, in which the systems of Buddhism, Hinduism, Jainism, Lokāyata and Islamism have penetrated. "In this varied situation it is neither desirable nor feasible to prescribe uniform curriculum and standards of philosophy teaching in a democratic country like India," writes Murty.[28]

Though some of the dynamic experts of the UGC suggested writing a comprehensive history of philosophical ideas in India in the context of social, economic and political factors, Murty informs that nobody undertook the project. However there is a need to write the history of Indian philosophy from the standpoint of the thinkers than the system in the historical perspective.

Murty stands for the plurality of philosophical thinking. He says that either in the past or in the present times there was no single philosophy of "independent Indian identity". For him, even the same socio-political conditions do not yield or result in the same philosophical thinking. No doubt, in a particular period certain issues and problems arise but the solution may not be uniform. A civilization may have a kind of ideas evolved into a homogeneous unique philosophy, but no nation can claim that a particular kind of ideas and doctrines

---

[27] K. Satchidananda Murty, *Philosophy in India,* p. 168.

[28] Ibid., p. 170.

are of its own. Hence Murty departs from the idea and proposal of having a single philosophy of independent Indian identity.[29]

There is a lot of discussion on how philosophy is to be taught in the contemporary times in terms of, either thinker-wise or theme-wise. Similarly some teachers of philosophy argue that philosophy should be taught selecting some problems of philosophy or selective passages of philosophical classics. In accordance with the view of S. Radhakrishnan who urged that we must recognize the solidarity of philosophy with history, intellectual life and the social conditions, Murty says that philosophy should be learned from the historical perspective. For him histories of philosophy are more inclusive or comprehensive than the problem-oriented writing and learning. In Murty's words:

> Philosophy students must know that their subject has a long history both in the East and in the West. No system existed as such from the beginning; each evolved. All systematic thinking is historical; problems arise in a particular context. . . . A history of philosophy can show all this. There cannot be any separation between the systematic problematic approach and the historical approach in philosophy.[30] A right sort of history of philosophy is indeed philosophy.[31]
>
> To sum up, no course other than the history of philosophy can bring home to a beginner in this subject the variety of problems and solutions, the way schools and systems developed and interacted with other subjects (e.g. religion, science, mathematics), and how all this was due to the creative work of individual

[29] K. Satchidananda Murty, *Philosophy in India,* p. 173.

[30] Ibid., p. 179.

[31] Ibid., p. 180.

thinkers, being influenced by the work of their predecessors and influencing and influenced by their contemporaries and contemporary conditions. When the classics are studied with this background they will become more meaningful and alive. A right type of history of philosophy would give a historical perspective to the problems of moral and social philosophy, metaphysics and epistemology and show how to interpret and analyse some important methods and doctrines developed over the centuries.[32]

[32] K. Satchidananda Murty, *Philosophy in India*, pp. 180-81.

3

Metaphysics

METAPHYSICS is a part of philosophy that contains discussions about space and time, God and the other world, belief and faith, mystic and transcendental experiences, religious and spiritual matters, and many issues that are not related to phenomenal world and perception. Metaphysics means "beyond physics", the kind of discussion that related to mind and the non-perceived things, fate and reason comes under the arena of metaphysics.

In his existential conditions and world of experience, man does not satisfy himself with what is around him and what is perceived with senses. The impulse to know something beyond and the intellectual pursuit thereafter led to formation of metaphysics. As one of the human pursuits, metaphysics has been the heart of philosophy, in the sense that it is the underlined principle of mind to examine the unknown reason for the known reality. Though metaphysics in an important part of philosophy, many consider it useless, when man is surrounded with more immediate things to know and problems to solve. For Descartes metaphysics is the root of knowledge; but for Hume it contains nothing but sophistry and illusion, hence Hume comments that books on metaphysics should be burned.[1]

Philosophy has been the rational examination and evaluation of the foundations of belief and faith; and it

[1] W.E. Kennick (ed.), *Metaphysics*, p. 1.

evaluates ideas relating to everyday life associated with religious, political and social areas. Murty as a teacher of philosophy, though emphasized that philosophy teacher should concern about social issues of the contemporary times and concerned himself prominently about social philosophy, yet wrote on the issues related to metaphysics with wide scholarship of East and West, being trained in Sanskrit language and Vedāntic literature.

According to Murty even the contemporary man needs metaphysics. Metaphysics is also something to be used by man like the instruments produced out of the discoveries made or invented by scientists. The modern gadgets like radio, television, cellphone, etc. are also in use by ordinary man, though he is incapable of making them or repairing them. Similarly, Murty says that people appropriate the kind of metaphysics they like.

Tradition and culture also provide a kind of metaphysics that satisfies the craving of man; and people accept it, though they are not authors, without any inquiry into the notions. As long as it is useful and provides satisfaction, metaphysics is what Murty refers to the Śaṅkara's *naisargikoyam loka vyavahāraḥ* and Descartes "ordinary course of life" or "accustomed way of life".[2] He also points out that there are some people in whom metaphysics originates. Man's experiences in this world sometimes cause pain and sometimes pleasure; the failure and success, the interaction among persons and association with things, on such and such occasion make man to think beyond. Murty writes:

> Whatever standpoint we adopt, however far we can think, we find that there still can be another beyond. The fact that we always think within limits, within dimensions, indicates that there is something beyond these dimensions.[3]

---

[2] K. Satchidananda Murty, *Metaphysics, Man and Freedom*, p. 23.

[3] Ibid., p. 24.

Murty observes that man becomes metaphysical when he starts questioning "why" and "how" of things and persons exist, and when man tries to find out one's relationship with the universe. When man meditates upon the very existence of himself and when he starts to think about his limitations and the abundance of the universe, or tries to find out the meaning of life and life beyond, he is doing metaphysics. Murty remarks:

> To seek this which is beyond things, so that we may know them in the whole, is metaphysics.[4]

The routine and mundane life, and the same repeated experiences sometimes lead to boredom. When apparent changes and things, which are valuable, become meaningless and futile, then man thinks of everything surpassing the visible roots to the invisible causes, and tries to go beyond and think beyond. When all things, which ordinarily take place in life, are vain and futile, man starts to inquire whether there might be anything truly good or try to understand and find out the causes.

When man experiences fear, trouble, repulsion out of the existence in the world, and when decay and death lead man to reflect upon to reach higher state of life, he tries to convert this world of suffering and tries to attain another world. Murty writes that the ethical story of Yayāti, the Upaniṣadic dialogue of Yājñavalkya with his wife, the Buddha's four-noble-truths and Arjuna's anguish in the great battlefield of Kurukṣetra are the examples of man's despair in the world. Murty explains that the existential experiences are also the basis for the formation of metaphysics. He writes:

> Man is a man (a mortal being) because he begins to die as soon as he is born. Potential death has made man what he is; and yet by obscuring this fact he has

[4] K. Satchidananda Murty, *Metaphysics, Man and Freedom*, p. 26.

> to live and be. When confrontation with death brings this enigma of human existence into clarity, an essential situation is created. An essential situation dramatises the total situation of man — his being in the world — and forces him to face up to it, transcend it and reconcile himself to his mode of being through metaphysics.[5]

According to Murty, the need for metaphysics is of threefold: intellectual, linguistic and psychological.

INTELLECTUAL NEED FOR METAPHYSICS

In the history of mankind, as early as in the sixth century BC the Sophists have broken the beliefs and customs; however the Greek world-view has remained the same. The development of science after the Middle Ages has also caused for the breakdown of certain religious beliefs and secular views. During the sixteenth and seventeenth centuries people of one country travelled to other lands and came into contact with "heterogeneous beliefs and varying customs, and amidst the clash of cultures and conflict of beliefs", that led to the conclusion that all beliefs are without foundation.[6] This kind of existential predicament not only makes man to disbelief and doubt but also think further to formation of metaphysical ideas. Murty says, "Metaphysics is the result of inevitable and healthy human activity."[7]

LINGUISTIC NEED FOR METAPHYSICS

There are several languages in the world, similarily there are several levels in a language spoken; for example the scientific language, the poetic language, the common man's language and religious language. Therefore, when there are different

[5] K. Satchidananda Murty, *Metaphysics, Man and Freedom*, p. 36.

[6] Ibid., p. 5.

[7] Ibid., p. 8.

levels in language why not we have a metaphysical language, argues Murty. He remarks that the metaphysical language can serve to co-ordinate the other levels of languages to become more meaningful. In other words, certain words like God and Being are needed to serve and tie-up all the levels of language.

PSYCHOLOGICAL NEED FOR METAPHYSICS

According to Murty, metaphysics is not scepticism; it would not lead a person to hopelessness. On the other hand, it provides the reflective understanding of the universe and life. He writes:

> Metaphysics is never realized in its plenitude; one never knows all the absolute presuppositions, and one often mistakes a fact or a misinterpretation of a fact to be an absolute presupposition. Absolute presuppositions are presuppositions implicated in all experiences and existence, in their various modalities and expressions. They are thus the depths of being, the core of the ultimate.[8]

Metaphysics is not a science to propose new facts, according to Murty, but "it is an interpretation of all that is known". It reveals our potentiality and freedom of thinking about the future and illuminates our existence by showing the limitation of our comprehension. People of different places will have different metaphysical conceptions, and also they change from time to time. Metaphysics constitutes faith and scheme, which establish a relation between finite and Infinite. A believer of a set of metaphysical outlook does not fall into nihilism or fatalism. A sinner, who has belief in some sort of metaphysics, even at the time of death, will aspire for an Infinite life after death or get tranquillity by following the required fulfilments.

---

[8] K. Satchidananda Murty, *Metaphysics, Man and Freedom*, p. 14.

MURTY'S INTERPRETATION OF THE SELF

Murty writes that man can be understood and interpreted in two ways: as a rational being (psychology) and an evolved being (anthropology). As a rational being, man has been conceived as a pure self-consciousness being that possesses an inward principle beyond temporal and spacious limitations, which is close to the interpretation of man in Vedāntic thought.

Murty says that, as an evolved being, man is a changing entity, having freedom, experiencing the events and inculcating the possibilities. Murty says that man can be understood completely when his being in the world and craving for the transcendental are better understood. The phenomenological experiences related to one's own self and of world, his meditations on the other world or the potentialities in realizing his relationship to Being are to be synthesized to know about man.

Murty says that man is to be understood with reference to actuality and potentiality. Actually man lives in the world, experiences the world, he belongs to some country and some culture at a particular time. It is also believed that there is no common nature in man and the behaviour of an individual relates to his tradition; this led to the conclusion that man can be understood and perceived in different types, namely the "medieval man" and the "Renaissance man". Contrary to this established facts and notions, the recent discoveries in anthropology began to reveal "similarities and resemblances in human behaviour and customs, in social organization and ethical and religious ideas among different tribes and culture all over the world".[9]

Even in the anthropological evolutionary status, man is in accordance with what the psychological nature of man is. In

[9] K. Satchidananda Murty, *Metaphysics, Man and Freedom*, p. 51.

spite of all variations the anthropological study is revealing the universal themes, fundamental elements and general picture of mankind. In whatever culture one is born, the adult man of every culture has possessed a number of sentiments and ideas, which are very much similar. The point to be noted is that man, as a particular person in a culture of a particular period in a particular place, seems to be different from that of others. But the abstract man, who is endowed with reason and self-consciousness alienates himself from the physical world, craves for the world beyond. Murty puts it:

> But in this inquiry he also gains inkling that there is something which he cannot know — at least the world as the whole, which is not in the world. The fact that he can at least have an inkling of this suggests he can in some way transcend the knowable world, though he cannot endure there. He finds himself to be situated in the knowable world and history but having the occasional privilege of going beyond it and roaming in the unknowable world that hovers round the knowable.[10]

The other aspect of understanding the concept of man, according to Murty, is that the inclination to search and to know that, which is beyond the perceivable world of experience after understanding one's own self. Man has learned in the beginning that he is a rational being, superior to all other beings in the world. His instincts differ from the animal instincts and thus man became a being endowed with spirit.

The psychological, anthropological and theological explanations have brought up a complete picture of man. If man thinks himself alone and limits his relations to the noumena or the world beyond, he remains an abstract or unreal man. Therefore, Murty says that the "real man must be known in

[10] K. Satchidananda Murty, *Metaphysics, Man and Freedom*, p. 44.

his relationship with other men".[11] The early researches asserted that there is no common human nature as there are many different ideas, customs and practices among different tribes at various places; but subsequently they revealed the similarities and resemblances, whatever the tradition may be. In this context Murty says, as earlier noted, being born in a tradition man has to live in the tradition, if he transcends his tradition he has to adopt another tradition; "to escape tradition completely is to annihilate oneself".[12]

MAN AND INDIVIDUALITY

Man and his relations with other persons in the society also constitute a part in the self-reflection of man. Man as a social being, in his understanding of other men, considers himself as a specific person and unique by considering all his inclinations, wishes, ideals and reflective attitudes as different. These self-reflections result in freedom of man thinking about himself, choosing whatever he likes, and taking a new path of life. Precisely, Murty writes:

> Self-reflection enables man not only to distinguish himself from others, inasmuch as he is conscious of certain actions and thoughts as "his" and his only.[13]

This self-reflection also makes man to arrive at the conclusion that the self is not the body; but in everyday life one has to identify his self with the body, as the self cannot be found without the body. Murty defines the self as follows:

> The self of a man is his individuality, the organisms' total response to the others and things.[14]

[11] K. Satchidananda Murty, *Metaphysics, Man and Freedom,* p. 50.

[12] Ibid., p. 53.

[13] Ibid., p. 55.

[14] Ibid., p. 56.

The point is that though the self is not the body, a person cannot think of his body without the self, therefore the self is not an object of perception; not only that, the self which thinks of other selves will also think about itself. Murty asserts the dialogue of the self in its self-reflection:

> The self in knowing itself, in approving or disapproving itself, in glorifying or condemning itself, is holding a conversation in itself.[15]

This is evident from our judgement of our self; it means the self, which judges other selves also judges itself; thus the self, at the same time, is the judge and the judged. The self, being a mystery to it, develops gradually since the birth influenced by social forces — culture, community and education apart from its native capacity of perception. The society, as a whole, moulds man according to its patterns, thus the developed man is the manifestation of culture. Man, being a product of social and physical conditions, in turn, tries to transform, to the extent possible, the social conditions, if not the physical environment. Murty writes:

> Of all things in the world we find that only man can develop, transmit and acquire culture, thus transforming himself and his offspring into self conscious individuals, with distinct attitudes, norms, skills and self-control. And only man has the capacity to govern what he produces.[16]

After trying to understand one's own self, man's inclination to know the beyond or world beyond and his relation with the society, man as a thinking being, and reflective person tries to understand nature, which is inexhaustible for human knowledge. Nature is that one which is real, and it is a

---

[15] K. Satchidananda Murty, *Metaphysics, Man and Freedom*, p. 61.

[16] Ibid., pp. 64-65.

precondition to human existence and survival. It is beyond human knowledge; probably there was nature when man was not or there might be nature before man existed. Murty says:

> Nature is the totality of things, capable of being perceived and determined by the general laws, discovered and discoverable by science.[17]

Murty concludes that all our problems come and interpretations arise due to lack of scientific approach in understanding nature. In other words all the problems and contradictions in understanding nature have been the result of the emphasis made on human-cognition or self-consciousness as the sole criterion for knowing truth, and even nature. But the nature is inexhaustible and beyond human cognition; in the nature man appeared, evolved and became a being of cognition and self-consciousness. Therefore the truth is that the depths of the nature cannot be known fully; and it is not possible to explain nature with human terms. Murty writes that nature is nothing but the world as a whole, including the comprehensible and the incomprehensible. Being part of nature, man cannot be against nature, thus man is phenomena logically bounded.

The dualism of the self and body has been an erroneous idea, according to Murty. He writes:

> A notional division of man into the self and the body can be legitimately made, but to take them as two distinct entities of the same ontological status, and then to analyse the self into the witness self and the self that acts and enjoys, identifying the former alone with the essence of man, is only a feat of abstraction.[18]

---

[17] K. Satchidananda Murty, *Metaphysics, Man and Freedom*, p. 68.

[18] Ibid., pp. 83-84.

Because of the dualism prevailed, man tried to escape from the body, thinking that the self as the eternal entity, in order to attain *mokṣa* or to get liberation from the finite world.

MOKṢA

The highest goal of man, according to Śaṅkarācārya, is *mokṣa* (liberation). It is the state of absolute freedom from ignorance (*avidyā*), unknowableness (*māyā*) and family life of suffering (*saṁsāra*). It is the state beyond the cycle of birth and death. Simply speaking, *mokṣa* is nothing but realization of the individual self as *Brahman*. According to Advaita Vedānta, *mokṣa* is not something to be achieved, but it is the very nature of the self. It is not something that follows after death, and it is not to be understood in the sense of endless existence in some distant and unknown world, it is the attainment of the highest state of consciousness through identifying the self (*ātmā*) and *Brahman*. It is to be attained here and now while one is still in one's bodily existence. In other words, it is the realization of non-difference of the individual self from the absolute Self. *Mokṣa* is called "experiencing non-duality" (*advaita-anubhava*). A man who attains such consciousness is called "the living free", *jīvan-mukta*. *Mokṣa* became the goal of man.

The nature of self, described by Murty is close to that of the analysis found in Vedānta. According to Murty, body is a necessary pre-condition for the actions to be performed, but thought and passion are associated with the self and cause the self to suffer, agitate and confront others. This state of the self, which is associated with thought and passion, leads one to perceive the self again without thought and passion. Murty says in sleeping state also the self is present but devoid of passion and thought; and in waking state the self also can be devoid of them by sitting on the judgement seat to consider what should be done, thought of and felt. Thus the self, described by Murty is a witnessing self (*sākṣī*), similar to the Vedāntic notion.

Apart from the Upaniṣadic states of the self, Murty divides the self as per the experiences into two kinds: (i) the witnessing self or the real self, and (ii) the agent self or the feeling self.[19] Murty writes that the witnessing self should be free from the feelings of choice, actions and results or consequences of guilt and sin, in order to attain freedom. In this context he reminds us for the first time, how the self is completely free from everything while in the world and nature, in the state of ecstasy.

The point that should not be forgotten is that no other philosopher has discussed and mentioned the ecstasy of the self, which expresses itself in many actions of the person in the mundane world. It is a fact, as Murty states, that the properties of some drugs, herbs and hot drinks, when taken, man experiences ecstasy. Even in the sexual act and also in dance one experiences ecstasy, the nature of which Murty describes as:

> In ecstasy, the self has neither memory, nor care. It abides in the pure present, freed from responsibility and thought and feeling of every kind, which might make it conscious of problems and relations. In ecstasy man is able to lift himself up from his finitude, i.e. he experiences no limitations.[20]

Murty on the basis of this experience of the self in the finite world infers the birth of the conception of the freedom of the self. If man disowns the human condition, a complete freedom will be possible for being in the physical nature; the self lost its freedom.

---

[19] K. Satchidananda Murty, *Metaphysics, Man and Freedom,* p. 75.

[20] Ibid., p. 76.

FREEDOM AS REVERSAL TO NORMAL LIFE

Murty says in this context, that the classical Indian philosophies have interpreted the apparent reality of the world or nature by denying its ontological status. Not only the existence of the world and the experiences of suffering, action, passion and thought have been denied but also normal movements and human conditions have been regulated. Spontaneous and conscious movements of man such as breathing, seeing and thinking have been regulated with introducing methods of meditation. The reason for this, as said above, is as follows, in Murty's own words:

> One does in it the reverse of what normal human beings do, on the assumption that the divine is the contradictory of the mundane.[21]

This kind of attitude culminated its abnormality; Murty puts in a precise way:

> This idea culminates in the conception that he who has succeeded in his efforts . . . will live in an abnormal way. As was said, all that is phenomenal is bondage; society and ethics are also therefore bondage. The liberated man cannot live normally, for the empirically normal man is in bondage. So the liberated man behaves abnormally. If normal man dresses, this man goes naked; if they cook and eat, he eats the dry leaves and grass; if they are afraid of the forest or the burial ground, he lives there.[22]

FREEDOM AS TRANSCENDING HUMAN RELATIONS

While, abrogate the human condition was one classical way of attaining freedom, the other way was to transcend life

---

[21] K. Satchidananda Murty, *Metaphysics, Man and Freedom*, p. 80.

[22] Ibid., p. 81.

while living in the world and society. This is known as the concept of the liberated man in life *(jīvan-mukta)* described in Advaita Vedānta.

The earlier step or way is to depart oneself from the society, whereas the later is alienating oneself while living in the society. One need not renounce the world but keep aloof from the business of the world, or should lead a mechanical life without involvement. This conception allows the fact that one has to reap the consequences of one's actions, or until the exhaustion one has to live a natural life in the world. This way of life has its basics in the dualism of the self and body in which the self is viewed as the witnessing self while the body indulges in actions. In other words, the assumption is that while the body involves in the world or while still continuing life in the world, the self remains untouched by the actions performed by the self. This is a state where man goes beyond the world and society.

Though Murty is well aware of the tradition and these two kinds of Indian philosophical perspectives advocated by the schools of the *Ṣaḍdarśana*s, he draws different implications. As said earlier, the division of man into self and body is a myth. Murty argues that either to consider man as pure self or to assert man as purely materialistic are both erroneous conclusions. One cannot treat the relation of body and self like oneself and his wife or his pen. One can renounce one's possessions but not his body. He writes:

> I cannot think of my body being without me. It is not a thing, which can be an object for me. For who am I when I consider it so? So it is not purely that of which I am conscious; nor is it definable as an X, which can be called mine. I cannot get rid of my body, without ceasing to be. So my relationship to my body is not external, it is not my possession. It is implied in me; and I am what form it. It is somewhat similar to the

> relationship between, say, a triangle and its three straight lines. Without three lines, there would not be a triangle; yet just three straight lines are not a triangle. A triangle is a special form, a unique structure, imposed on the lines; but the structure does not exist when the lines are not there.[23]

Therefore Murty argued that the division of self and body may be conceived but to take them as two distinct entities like a man and his wife or a person and his pen are intellectual gymnastics or "a flat of abstraction". In continuation of the same proposition, Murty writes that it is highly difficult for man to live in the transcendental world while living in the phenomenal world. The finite world has its source in the Infinite Being, which is transcendental. This fact implies that there is relation between the phenomenal and transcendental, between the finite and Infinite. Then it is impossible, Murty says, for man to transcend the world, as the transcendental Being is the ground of the world. Therefore, while living in the world, it is an impossible task — as advocated in some philosophies of India, for man to be beyond the world. He writes:

> To be in the world and to escape the laws of nature, to remain a man and yet not to be a finite existence in the world and in history, is — as the *Gītā* pointed out long ago — an impossibility.[24]

Freedom cannot be achieved either renouncing the world by seeking the opposite of what the normal man in society is doing nor restraining oneself or transcending from the day-to-day life of the world while living. On the other hand, according to Murty, man is endowed with freedom to think that one is bounded by the world is a false conception, for freedom, ultimately means the freedom to be what one

[23] K. Satchidananda Murty, *Metaphysics, Man and Freedom,* p. 59.

[24] Ibid., pp. 85-86.

conceives and wills. In this context Murty says that if one thinks that there are still some objectives, set by culture, to be achieved by one, he will not have freedom. Culture is man-made; there is no culture before man. The diversity of cultures in the world shows that culture does not remain stagnant. Culture is like agriculture and technology, which are changing and developing; which man invents shows that man is free. Psychologically speaking, men being egocentric sometimes defy and flout society when they will or set aside the pressures of society. Man has not remained slave to his instincts; even he suppressed some and created new ideas, formulated new goals. There are people who sacrificed their life for society; and also there are people who revolted against the social order and norms. He writes:

> It is the capacity of man to choose and determine his course of action. Of course, man acts culturally, historically, but no culture or tradition sets before men any single goal or objective, presents a single way of dealing with problems, or leading one's life. Still man chooses out of these, what he likes, and achieves them.[25]

The development in science and various forms of art — poetry, music, sculpture, literature and ideologies — presupposes the freedom of man and his potentiality to create new forms. Therefore to Murty, freedom is the realization of oneself "in his concrete living situation — as a finite existence involved in history, as the synthesis of a self and a body".[26]

Philosophy, as a spiritual contemplation, of action inspired by reason, acts purposively and creatively in the true sense, for we really act only when something occurs of which we are the adequate cause. Murty's explanation about the self is very

---

[25] K. Satchidananda Murty, *Metaphysics, Man and Freedom*, pp. 89-90.

[26] Ibid., p. 93.

near to the Vedāntic perspectives of Śaṅkara; however he departs from many popular explanations and explored new avenues. He not only speaks of relation between God and the world but also thinks that God is known and unknown. He dialectically maintains like Śaṅkara, bringing the opposite of the accepted popular notions. The thinking of Karl Jaspers, the existentialist, has influenced Murty while dealing with metaphysical problems of God, man and the world. Murty says:

> The noblest and most appropriate action in any domain — political or social — is . . . the highest exercise of the soul, contemplation of the spirit.[27]

Whether one accepts or not every human being consciously or unconsciously feels the sense of God. He writes that Pascal's statement "heavens and birds (i.e. nature) do not prove God" is similar to the Upaniṣadic saying, *tasyopaniṣad satyasya satyam iti* (the secret name of the transcendent is the truth of truth). To man, Pascal attributed three brilliant phrases — inconsistency, weariness and unrest. Because of suffering, tragic, despair and death are found everywhere in the world. When the constitutive principles of the divine reality (truth, beauty and goodness) exert their activity; then form faith, love and hope.

The concept of transcendent is mysterious because it is different from what is known and also from what is unknown. Murty critically analysed the condition of man and contemplation. Transcendent cannot furnish any doctrine, so the philosopher fabricates myths, parables and tales, which cannot be brushed aside easily. Though they have no scientific base and reason, stories of creation, the souls itinerary after death, conceptions of heaven and hell, God's covenant with men and his special intervention in physical form in human history are created, which are the examples of myths. They

---

[27] K. Satchidananda Murty, *An Exercise in Mystical Ontology*, Lucknow: Lucknow University, 1963, p. 1.

all seek not to teach, but disclose the mystery of the divine and man's obligation towards God.

Man is embedded with sufferings by natural catastrophes, human stupidity and the incurable evils of disease and death. The above things are the standpoint for a man to think about the eternal transcendent, thereby suffering and despair will be removed. Only by meditating on the boundlessness of divine reality and the transcendent, one can drive away the despair, and attain delight. Murty says:

> Delight (*ānanda*) is a principle of the Infinite, the boundless. . . .[28]

The highest wisdom is to realize delight. Murty says that it is the delight, which inspires the luminous mind of man. When the truth of this primal delight is realized, man is able to enjoy existence, and can taste the honeyed wave, which issues out of the ocean of bliss.

The *Ṛgveda* asserts about the wise man and the ignorant man, comparing them in a story of two inseparable birds sitting on a tree. One of them eats the sweet fruit of the tree and the other looks on. The above example implies that the wise man realizes the secret of delight, and the inner reality, by which all beings live. In this connection, Murty remarks:

> I do not follow traditional interpretations, which are not unanimous, nor are modern orientalists unanimous. Mostly traditional commentators following Yāska (XIV. 29) identify the two birds with soul and God and the tree with the body (*vṛścyata iti vṛkṣo dehaḥ* — Sāyaṇa). It is the universe, *saṁsāra,* which is usually spoken of as the tree in the Vedic literature. That sense is more appropriate here too.[29]

---

[28] K. Satchidananda Murty, *An Exercise in Mystical Ontology*, p. 5.

[29] Ibid., pp. 21f.

Eternity is immutability; God is ever what ought to be. He says:

> The world is the dance of Śiva; time is the rhythm and movement of this dance undertaken to express the abundance of dynamics and delight in him.[30]

Hence the word "contemplation" has been extensively used by Murty to explain the Infinite, which is to be meditated upon, in order to be out of suffering and to attain the unsurpassed happiness. Spiritual men always seek the good that satisfies and delights; they enjoy the supreme *rasa,* the *Brahman*; *rasa* is what gives contentment, peace and joy. That which is desired is good; that which is most dear and desired is the Supreme Good. Murty says:

> We are able to distinguish different degrees of goodness, construct a hierarchy of values and conceive the supreme as that which is desired for itself. What is dear for the sake of itself is the Supreme Good.[31]

For Murty, the realm of values is the kingdom of God. It extends over the whole world, it is glorious, splendid, unattainable by others, inseparable and worthy of worship. God's sovereignty protects and unifies; his kingdom is ruled in accordance with the holy law (*ṛta*), expressing the cosmic order. But God's kingdom is an eternal reality, which is ever present as a saving realm of the divine power and glory. Murty compares the God of Quran with that of Upaniṣadic God, i.e. which is beyond speech and reason, creator of all, ground and apex of all beings, but surpassing all, interpenetrating everything from within as the inner self.

---

[30] K. Satchidananda Murty, *An Exercise in Mystical Ontology*, p. 9.

[31] Ibid.

4

The Indian Spirit

PROF. Murty occupies a predominant place in the contemporary philosophical world. While discussing the philosophical conceptions, he projects the subject in an incredible way, with a scholarship of both Indian and Western philosophy. His spectrum of philosophy is far and wide, even extended to the Far East and Middle East. However his thought is completely Indian.

The loom of Indian culture is vast and warm, interspersed with big rivers emanating from the Himalayas and Western Ghāṭs creating vast plains in the north and deltas in the south. The cotton of this cloth is composed highly by cultured and semi-civilized people. In spite of numerous invasions, which have swept past the country, threatening the very basis of culture, it has remained unruffled.

In the formation and development of Indian culture, first, environment has played a significant role. Surrounded on the three sides by sea and ocean, having Himalayas on the north protecting people from the northern cold waves, watered by the holy rivers such as Ganges and Godāvarī, and with the green and fertile lands, the ancient Indian life was glorious. Nature has bestowed its fullest possible gifts upon India and decked the entire landscape with the best of the beauties that nature could possibly bestow.

Murty in *Hinduism and Its Development* and *The Indian Spirit* has brought out the spirit of India by studying its civilization, culture and thought. A number of Western Orientalists and Indologists have interpreted that Indian culture was predominantly mystical, other-worldly; and that Indians do not have the sense of history and never bothered about injustice, oppression, poverty and life on earth. Even the Indian scholars have projected that India was a land of spiritualism, and renunciation, detachment and *mokṣa* were considered the sole aims of Indian life and perspective. Keeping in view of these statements that reflected only one shade of Indian life and thought, Murty in these books presents the totality of Indian spirit.

These books, especially *The Indian Spirit*, were written as academic responses to the charges made against Indian culture. Murty has shown that India's history, philosophy, the social, moral and spiritual ideas, and values have an immense value and importance not only for Indians but also for the citizens of the world as a whole. The Indian spirit has been presented not on the basis of the existing beliefs and stream of thought but facts of Indian life, practices and forgotten evidences in the existing classical literature, which was acclaimed by one and all. N.K. Devaraj writes:

> I received your excellent book *The Indian Spirit* over a week back, and have been reading it. You write like "Radhakrishnan in *Free India*", without any sense of apology or in any purely defensive spirit. One marvels at your versatile talent and amazingly wide sweep of information. You are truly suited to the role of the "Cultural Ambassador of India".[1]

INDIAN CULTURE

Murty says that culture is an attempt to realize certain fundamental values in social life. Every culture in its

---

[1] K. Ramakrishna Rao et al. (eds.), *Collected Criticism of K. Satchidananda Murty*, pp. 175-76.

development is confronted with stagnation and disintegration; hence culture changes and evolves. As human nature and aspirations are same everywhere, cultural change takes place.

To know the culture of India one must start with the study of civilization of the Moheñjo-Dāṛo and Haṛappā. Whether it is relevant or not, the Vedas should not be forgotten, for they are no way obstacles for progress. The *Ṛgveda* and the *Atharvaveda* do not anywhere mention this world as a place of suffering and as something to be escaped. Murty writes that thoughtful living men, according to the circumstances, articulate the culture of their own. He writes:

> Culture is not like a bloodless mathematical system, completely coherent and logical. Like a great painting or music, it contains a blending of discordant elements fused together in a manner which defies description.[2]

Culture needs interchanging of ideas, thoughts and progressive work without disturbing the already existing systems. Any great culture, either European or Indian contains more than one strand. Indian culture is over 5,000 years old and has emerged in an organic manner throughout the ages, getting enriched by intermixing of several races, religions and cultures, while its basic structure was founded during the Vedic period of Indian history. It has developed, grown, spread and enriched itself all through the successive centuries. In this context Murty says that Indian cultural development should not be identified exclusively with Āryanization or Islamic impact or Westernization. On the other hand, the archaeological discoveries at Mohenjo-Dāṛo and Haṛappā revealed that some of the aerial gods in Vedic culture and heritage have their origin in this great culture and civilization.

---

[2] K. Satchidananda Murty, *The Indian Spirit*, p. 29.

With reference to the evolution of Indian culture, Murty has accepted the historical, anthropological and sociological doctrines and interpreted them in a scientific approach, which seems to be more rational and logical, different from the traditional point of view. Though the Āryans conquered India and established their sovereignty over the land, their culture was subsequently influenced by Draviḍian elements and ways of life; and thus synthesis and fusion of the contradictory ways of life emerged. He writes:

> The Āryan and Draviḍian worked together and there emerged from this conjoint endeavour, a distinct cultural pattern of life and thought-Hinduism.[3]

Modern Indian culture has its basis in ancient Indian thought and life as viewed in Sanskrit literature. Majority of the modern Indians consider that what is maintained in them is the best standard. Objectively speaking, Indian culture has been a complex one sustained with other forms of culture apart from the Sanskrit aspirations and inspirations, says Murty.

He is of the opinion that Indian people and their culture cannot be understood by simply studying limited books produced before sixth century BC related to a minority community of the total Indian population, dealing with the doctrines of *Brahman* and the concept of *dharma*.[4] The misunderstanding of Indian culture is the result of the Western and Indian scholars' interpretation, who tried to understand Indian culture on the basis of theological books that were produced in the middle ages of Indian history without any knowledge of the books related to art and history, astronomy and mathematics, medicine and sex.

---

[3] K. Satchidananda Murty, *Hinduism and Its Development*, p. 79.

[4] K. Satchidananda Murty, *The Indian Spirit*, p. 4.

Murty says that Indian culture and civilization of the present day is neither unchanging nor making progress in full spirit. The modern Indian is equally like that of a modern man of Greece and Italy to his ancient times. There is change in Indian culture and at the same time inheritance of the past:

> Man is a free spirit; whenever he becomes aware of his condition, he can remake, remould, reform and revolutionize his own personality as well as that of his culture and society.[5]

Murty says that Indian culture is humanistic in the sense that man is given importance among beings in the terrestrial world. According to almost all the Indian philosophies and scriptures, man stood at the apex of the ascending order of the manifestation of beings in the world. Śaṅkarācārya in his book *Vivekacūḍāmaṇi* explains that to born as human being is a rare and great opportunity. In his analysis of Indian culture, Murty has advanced a progressive outlook about philosophies and religions. For him, Hinduism has its own religious humanism like that of Christianity and Buddhism, though differs from the humanism of Renaissance.

Murty remarks that spiritual expression in Hindu philosophy is equal to that of any other philosophy or philosophical theology. India cannot be called as a country of spiritualism alone contrary to the developed nations of the West, materialistically as the European countries gave birth to a number of Christian saints. Similarly China and Japan cannot be considered as less spiritualistic than India as they were the homelands of Taoism and Zen Buddhism.[6] The reason for the assertion of spirituality in Indian culture by Indian scholars, according to Murty, is due to two reasons. First, Indian scholars understood the superiority of the West in social

[5] K. Satchidananda Murty, *The Indian Spirit*, p. 94.

[6] Ibid., p. 6.

and political matters, industry and technology that took place in the nineteenth century. Second, there was lack of an authentic information and writings of ancient Indians with reference to political thought and historical perspective, economics and mathematics, medicine and sexology. Therefore the Indian writers placed importance on the scriptures that dealt with spirituality and other worldliness by laying emphasis on renunciation (*saṁnyāsa*) and liberation (*mokṣa* or *nirvāṇa*) to assert the superiority of Indian culture.[7]

The implication is that, according to Murty, either spiritualism or atheism or pantheism or materialism was not the viewpoint of any country or nation. He says:

> Human nature, I maintain, is uniform all over the world; and even as empirical experience and science, the metaphysical and mystical experiences of mankind have common features which do not allow us to brand any particular types of these as especially "Western" or "Eastern".[8]

Therefore he says that it is silly to compare which one is the higher philosophy or religion to the other. Further, he writes:

> To be a Hindu one need not believe in God, or even the Absolute, as the Advaita Vedāntins do.[9]

The history of India reveals that efforts were made to perceive its culture from the aggressor's point of view. Hinduism, as a faith, is a way of life and many-sided — all things to all men; it is hardly possible to define it, or indeed to say definitely whether it is a religion or not, in the usual sense of the word. In its present form, and even in the past, it embraces many

---

[7] K. Satchidananda Murty, *The Indian Spirit*, p. 4.

[8] Ibid., p. 7.

[9] Ibid., p. 190.

beliefs and practices, from the highest to the lowest, of those opposed each other or contradicting one another. Murty remarks:

> Hinduism itself cannot be considered to be the only authentic philosophy of India; Cārvāka, Buddhism, Jainism and Sikhism are as much Indian as Hinduism, and since Islam and Christianity have been appropriated by Indians for centuries now, they too are authentically Indian.[10]

India is a vast subcontinent having diversity in geographical, cultural, ethnic and religious traits on the one hand; and on the other hand, it has unity, which is something deep and indefinable. Murty is a great optimist and visualizes as follows:

> India . . . has much greater difficulties to surmount because of its vast population, the caste system, lesser national integration, lesser resources and economic under-development. . . . If India could establish a free and just society and abolish the shocking contrasts of wealth and poverty and extend the minimum benefits of modern civilization to all its citizens, it would be fulfilling its destiny.[11]

World Affirming

In general, some Western writers and Indian thinkers consider renunciation (*saṁnyāsa*) as the highest of the four life-stages (*āśrama*s) of man. Again to discuss objectively, Murty reveals the fact that the four life-stages were neither applicable to all nor prescribed to all according to the Indian scriptures. It is a norm according to the Brāhmanical books but not a practice in the society, he writes. The Vedas do not speak about the four life-stages. The world was never mentioned as a place of

---

[10] K. Satchidananda Murty, *The Indian Spirit*, pp. 140-41.

[11] Ibid., p. 52.

suffering. *Saṁnyāsa* and *mokṣa* were never mentioned as the goals of life in the *Ṛgveda*. The Vedic *ṛṣis* (sages) wanted to live hundreds of years with good health and wealth, described life on earth more than heavenly life, and most of them are married men. Murty informs:

> Contentment with one's lot, indifference to material prosperity, precepts to limit one's wants — these are not found in the Vedas. Even in the Upaniṣads, *Brahma-jñānīs* (knowers of *Brahman*) were not averse to riches, good food and married life; some of them sought these actively.[12]

The Mīmāṁsā School, particularly Kumārila, the interpreter of the Vedas, opposed the idea of renunciation. It is a fact that renunciation (*saṁnyāsa*) was an ideal for limited schools of India and was made fashionable due to the teachings and the life of the Buddha and Mahāvīra; and in the Middle Ages, Śaṅkarācārya advocated it. Therefore, Murty says that culture includes ideals and facts, and the life as lived by a people and thoughts as articulated by them. He believes that the greatness of India is basically due to its culture, which blends "this worldliness" and "other worldliness" in a unique manner.

In general any philosopher in India does not neglect the tradition; the present scenario of human life is already embodied at the roots of the tradition. Murty says that progress of a country or state is possible, even without having a notion of what the progress means. If progress is the means of the absence of wars, the great two world wars and the cold war in the last century disproved the definition for that there has been a tremendous progress in the twentieth century. Though not yet proved, if progress is the result of the rapport that exists among religions and the type of society that exists, Hinduism does not contribute for the backwardness of the country. He remarks:

---

[12] K. Satchidananda Murty, *The Indian Spirit*, p. 10.

> Any way, there is nothing in Hinduism which impedes progress, democracy, science and material prosperity; on the contrary, Hindu culture is more favourable to them than some others.[13]

The exclusive study of the Vedas and the Upaniṣads and the sayings of the Buddha and the writings of Śaṅkarācārya made the world to believe that Indian scholarship is something religious and metaphysical aimed at salvation — *nirvāṇa* or *mokṣa.* But the Indian texts written by Kauṭilya, Varāhamihira, Caraka and Vātsyāyana dealing with political economy, astronomy, medicine and sexology, respectively, affirm the positive side of Indian culture.

The sayings of the Vedas are world-affirmative and wealth-oriented. The Vedic prayers contain the desire for long life of 100 years. The Vedic people desired *soma* (wine), meat, chariots, horses, etc. According to the Upaniṣads, the sage Yājñavalkya was a lover of beef and wealth; and he had two wives — Maitreyī and Kātyāyanī. The great sage Raikva taught knowledge after accepting a princess, dowry and lands. In the Upaniṣads, most *ṛṣis* lived with families in the hermitages, *tapovanas* (forests of penances).

A study of Indian classical literature shows that no people were practical in this world than the Indians, who were fond of material prosperity and power, delight and sensual pleasures. Vātsyāyana's *Kāmasūtra,* a book on the "principles and practice of love" describes the art of sex or love-making. The Hindu temples, mostly, contain sculptures of love-making, at least in one corner or side of the temple; especially in the Purāṇic literature there was a God of sex in the Hindu pantheon of gods and goddesses. In this context, Murty writes:

---

[13] K. Satchidananda Murty, *The Indian Spirit,* p. 81.

> Good food (*pañca bhakṣya, ṣaḍrasa*), gold and diamonds, silks and scents, *aiśvarya* and *vaibhava*, power and glory, are the themes which are recurrent in Indian secular and religious art and literature.[14]

Basically, Murty is a literary trial blazer while dealing with metaphysical aspects, both Indian and Western. For him, the historical background of the Indian spirit lies in the comprehensiveness of its systems and thereby to elaborate things in a lucid manner. The Western thinkers fail to understand the mind of Indian thought, thinking that it is purely mystic and other-worldliness. He points out:

> If Kauṭilya, Brahmagupta and Varāhamihira, Caraka and Vātsyāyana had received as much attention as the writers of the Upaniṣads, the Buddha and Śaṅkara from competent European and Indian scholars, the picture of India in both modern Western and Eastern minds would have been different.[15]

The message of Hinduism, according to Murty, is not to renounce the world but to enjoy the world. Since the self (*ātman*) is *ānandamaya,* life is a dynamic enjoyment and attainment of positive bliss. The eternal bliss comes when all doubts are resolved and fears are scattered. Amidst of fields and cities, cinemas and classes, machines and markets man has to be in calm and unruffled. He writes:

> Hinduism asks us to take our full share in the struggles and aspirations, the toils and turmoils of humanity. There is no use of our continuing to be in the world without taking any interest in it. We should not be living-corpses, *jīvan-mṛta*s. We should be intensely active taking part in the movements of the world. . . .[16]

---

[14] K. Satchidananda Murty, *The Indian Spirit*, p. 58.

[15] Ibid., p. 5.

[16] K. Satchidananda Murty, *Hinduism and Its Development*, p. 59.

Murty remarks that the conservative belief and faith in a set of dogmas has lead to the conflict between different religions in the past. For example, the concept of "chosen people" of Judaism, which later influenced Christianity and Islam, has become the poisonous germ resulting in hatred and Crusades. On the contrary Hinduism as stated in the previous pages has been the religion of different cults and creeds with various kinds of interpretations. Thus the pluralistic aspect has been the centre of gravity of Hinduism because "Hinduism begins and ends in *anubhava*".[17] In the end, Murty categorically declares:

> I do not know which "the key" is, if there is one, for understanding Indian culture, but it is certainly not total indifference to history. No other culture was more concerned with this world, with material prosperity and sensual pleasures than Indian culture.[18]

CASTE SYSTEM

Since the dawn of Vedic literature, Indian writers believed and outlined the *catur* (four) aspects of *varṇa-vyavasthā* (caste system), *āśrama-dharma*s (values of life stages) and *puruṣārthas* (human goals). Murty has interpreted the origin and development of the *caturvarṇa-vyavasthā* (four-caste system), in a scientific way admitting the anthropological and historical facts. He says that the scheme of four *varṇa*s was originated in a pastoral society by accommodating all people. The four *varṇa*s or types of groups at first were based on birth and capacity, but in later time birth alone came to determine one's *varṇa*. So man's *svabhāva* or his inclinations and capacities were replaced with heredity and selfishness. Subsequently, due to

---

[17] K. Satchidananda Murty, *Hinduism and Its Development*, p. 20.

[18] K. Satchidananda Murty, *The Indian Spirit*, p. 41.

inclusion of various tribes and people into the Hindu fold the caste system has been formed.[19]

The learned brāhmaṇas of the Vedas were held in high esteem; while the ordinary priests, who were involved in performing the ceremonies of marriages, births and deaths, were equally treated with middle classes. The ancient Indian texts like the *Bṛhat-kathā*, *Pañcatantra* and other folk classical literature like *kāvya*s and *nāṭaka*s reveal this fact.[20] Murty also says that the brāhmaṇas were placed in higher position in the scriptures, but it was not a fact as a variety of rulers and merchants have attained prominence. The history of India testifies that when the trading guilds and classes became powerful by establishing Mauryan, Śuṅga and Gupta empires, the brāhmaṇas and kṣatriyas joined together for supremacy. On the other hand, when the repeated invasions weakened the rulers, the commercial and the priestly classes gained power; hence the priestly classes glorified the new arrivals into India. Therefore in the medieval times, kṣatriyas joined together with brāhmaṇa orthodoxy.[21]

Murty says that caste system is responsible for two developments.[22] First, each caste remained a unit and developed its own ethics, customs and ideas by sacrificing universal ethics applicable to all men. Caste gained importance and the individual rights have been undermined. Second, due to ban on the change of occupation and *karma* theory, man became a spectator. Therefore no revolutions occurred in the history of India.

The *varṇa* system depicts kṣatriyas as kings or rulers of the land; but the history of India shows many kings of India

---

[19] K. Satchidananda Murty, *The Indian Spirit*, p. 196.

[20] Ibid., pp. 13-14.

[21] Ibid., p. 198.

[22] Ibid., pp. 199-200.

were not kṣatriyas as the great Pāṇḍavas and Mauryans and many later kings had "Śūdra blood or often non-Indian blood in them".[23] But it is also a fact that the ordinary śūdras' position was similar to that of slaves in ancient Greece and Roman empires. Murty also points out that, contrast to the caste system, the Hindu scriptures emphasize universal ethics. The *Ṛgveda* says that the creator of the universe is the father of all men. Speaking truth, filial pigsty, respect towards gods and teachers, hospitality, non-injury are the virtues meant for all according to the Upaniṣads. The *Bhagavad-Gītā* speaks about the "welfare of all beings" (*sarvabhūta hitam*) and "friendliness and compassion to all beings" (*sarvabhūtanam maitraḥ karuṇā*).

SENSE OF HISTORY

Philosophy of history is a study that tries to reveal the underlying principles that guide the course of history, and thus various interpretations emerge while writing the histories of human societies or countries. Amaury de Riencourt, a Frenchman, who tried to interpret Indian history in his book, *The Soul of India,* draws the attention of Murty.

Riencourt, as a whole, while unveiling the "Indian soul" had made strange remarks about Indian mentality, stating that Indians never cared for history and historical studies. He argued, "Indians have non-unified egos, split or multiple personalities within single individuals".[24] As a whole for Riencourt, Indians always look back to find glorious chapters in their history, which may be called as an imagined ideal state of the past, advocated "ruthless cynical politics divorced from morality" and without a perspective of unity. In this context Murty presents certain facts about Indian history and society to evolve and comprehend the other side that was ignored by Riencourt.

---

[23] K. Satchidananda Murty, *The Indian Spirit*, p. 14.

[24] Ibid., p. 39.

Murty points out that it has been the universal phenomena prevailed among many nations, to get inspiration from the past. Rousseau had idealized the life of the "noble savages", the classical age of the Greece was considered ideal during Renaissance, and Mussolini aspired the resurgence of Roman glory. Therefore, belief in the concept of *Rāma-rājya* among Indians is in no way different from that of the other ideals. Murty also says that Kauṭilya of India has his counterparts in Europe — especially Machiavelli, Bismarck, Meinecke and Croce. Hence he argues that anyone who has soaked himself in a tradition, widely travelled and read with empathy can understood well.[25]

Though India did not have the comprehensive history of the whole of India as the West or Europe, Murty writes, there is a good deal of record occasionally in the history relating to some cultural history of tribes, castes and communities. The temples at Purī, Śrīraṅgam and other places maintained the past records of the visits of rich pilgrims and also their charities to the temple. The astronomer Āryabhaṭṭa and the physician Caraka had developed advanced theories, while the temples of Ellorā, Koṇārka and Mahābalipuram speak of the developed engineering of the ancient Indians. Biographers of some kings and religious teachers, histories of temples and monasteries were written in ancient India. Kalhaṇa's *Rājataraṅginī* depicts the history of the kings of Kashmir, and the *Mahāvaṁśa* contains a record history of Sri Lanka. The Vedas and Upaniṣads illustrate the courts of ancient Indian kings like Janaka of Videha, Ajātaśatru of Kāśī; and the stories of kings Janamejaya and Bharata were also mentioned. The life and activities of Kṛṣṇa were recorded in the *Bhāgavatam, Harivaṁśam* and *Mahābhārata;* the life of the Buddha was in the Piṭakas and Pāli

---

[25] K. Satchidananda Murty, *The Indian Spirit*, p. 50.

books, while the life of Śaṅkarācārya was in the Śaṅkara-vijayas.[26]

Murty says that the Itihāsa–Purāṇas are not less historical than the books of the Bible. He recalls how facts were invented, remoulded and arranged to fit into a pattern of approved apparent realities. However Indians, he affirms, do have the sense of history and the progress of the society from age to age.

Murty writes that according to Hindu beliefs, God is active in history; in the *Bhagavad-Gītā* it is said that God incarnates in every age to protect the righteous and punish the evil ones. In other words, Hindus believe in incarnation (*avatāra*) of God in every age to maintain the world-welfare, *loka-saṁgraha.* According to the Hindu Purāṇas, there have been ten great *avatāras*. Buddhism believes in twenty-four incarnations of the Buddha; and the coming Buddhāvatāra is Maitreya. Belief in ages of varying degrees, cyclically succeeding each other, is also the predominant characteristic of Indian tradition. The Kṛtayuga is the age of enlightenment and righteousness, which symbolizes the era of Vikramāditya, with peace and prosperity. The Kaliyuga is the age of ignorance and evil, marked with poverty, wars, oppression and cruelty. The Tretāyuga is said to be the reign of Rāma whose law creates the kingdom of heaven on earth, *Rāma-rājya.*[27]

There are certain popular beliefs clarified by Murty with reference to Indian history. It has been assumed that Āryans were superior to Draviḍians, the natives of ancient India; and the Āryans have civilized the inferior races and tribes of India. But Murty brings into light that the hero of the Mahābhārata war, Kṛṣṇa and the writer of the great epic of India, Vedavyāsa

---

[26] K. Satchidananda Murty, *The Indian Spirit*, pp. 55-56.

[27] Ibid., pp. 61-63.

were not Āryans. He interprets and remarks that colonization and conquests will not bring greater changes in the culture of any nation for culture itself changes from time to time. However, it seems that every country and nation in the world have been invaded and conquered by other country or nation, and each has been benefited by the other.[28]

Murty also points out that, in spite of the existence of smaller kingdoms in ancient India, there has been a vision for greater India, "akhaṇḍa Bhārat". The ancient sages and kings desired to become the great emperor of the whole of India; and the kings not only performed the Rājasūya-yajña, but also undertook the tour of invasions in the name of *dig-vijaya*s to establish a unified India.[29]

SOCIAL THOUGHT

Predomination of religion in ethical values is one of the chief characteristics of Indian culture, according to Murty, though his conclusions differ. He argues that ancient scriptures of India are "this-worldly" than any other religious literature. Hindus gave greater importance to the pleasures of this world and prominence to the empirical experiences.

In order to understand the spirit of any culture or country one has to consider the whole literature without limiting to a particular set of classical texts. Murty writes that one should not make any general assertions and propositions by taking isolated passages and utterances of monks and mystics.[30] The conceptions of *dharma,* belief in *karma, varṇa* theory and life after death or salvation (*mokṣa*) have influenced the Hindu thought and life. In the Vedas the word *ṛta* represents the cosmic order or law of the universe and the word *dharma* is

[28] K. Satchidananda Murty, *The Indian Spirit,* p. 66.

[29] Ibid., p. 67.

[30] Ibid., p. 80.

the counterpart of it in ethical values. *Dharma* is virtue, good, moral convention, law and religion. As a whole, *dharma* is nothing but the desirable actions prescribed by Vedic injunctions, and violation of it leads to chaos and resultant misery. This led the Hindu mind further to conceive and believe the *karma* theory or the law of causation in actions and their results, according to which good actions result in better fruits while bad actions lead to worst conditions. In other words, according to the *karma* theory the present actions, state and life are the result of past actions in the earlier life or birth, and the future-birth depends upon the present. However, though mechanical and cyclical the *karma* theory seems to be, by the grace of God or sincere repentance or by performing virtuous actions or penance, man is free to make and remould his destiny. The *karma* theory binds one to his caste and to the profession ordained to it, which is a *svadharma*. Thus the metaphysical *karma* theory provides basis for social classification of men.[31]

Indian religions never glorified the state of being poor; beggars and lazy people have no place in Hinduism. Begging is limited to those who are engaged in spiritual pursuits like religious mendicants (*bhikṣus* or *saṁnyāsins*) but not to the public.[32] Gifts to learned priests and *puṇḍits* are encouraged, the kings, princess and brāhmaṇas and as well as the gods were depicted in luxury in the ancient literature. Indian culture has glorified neither kings nor soldiers but lawgivers and saints.

The Hindu ethics is in tune with socialism, says Murty, than capitalism or communism. The great sage Tulasīdās taught that all the wealth belongs to Rāma, the Lord God of the great Indian epic, the *Rāmāyaṇa;* some popular songs describe that the land belongs to Lord Kṛṣṇa, God of the great Indian epic,

---

[31] K. Satchidananda Murty, *The Indian Spirit*, p. 194.

[32] Ibid., p. 83.

the *Mahābhārata.*[33] The modern Indian thinkers like Ranade, Raja Rammohun Roy, M.N. Roy, Vivekananda, Vinoba Bhave, Subhas Chandra Bose, Jawaharlal Nehru, Jayaprakash Narayan and Rammanohar Lohia were the ardent advocates of socialism in one form or the other.[34]

The Vedic sentences, the *Manusmṛti,* the *Mahābhārata,* the *Arthaśāstra* of Kauṭilya, the *Nītiśāstra* of Śukrācārya (*Śukra-nīti*) and many books of ancient Hindu culture have depicted ethics and politics. The form of government in the Vedic times was monarchy; but the king listened to the people's assemblies called *sabhā* and *samiti.* [35] In later Vedic times the word *pariṣad* came into use, in which poets and *puṇḍits* used to take part. Though the crown seems to be hereditary, the *Mahābhārata* admits the election of kings as well as the throwing of unfit kings. The Hindu lawgiver Manu asserts the right of the people to revolt against the oppressive king.

The government came into existence, according to the *Mahābhārata,* probably for two reasons. Either the original good ancient society might have been demoralized later or the ancient society might have been a lawless society. Therefore the result of both the reasons was the creation of a king to maintain law and order. Murty categorically states that according to ancient Hindu thinkers the business of the government was to maintain justice, which was nothing but individual's performance of *svadharma* or the rules pertaining to caste, family, religion and the country. Punishment (*daṇḍa*) was enforced to keep it up.

The *Śatapatha Brāhmaṇa* states that the ruler is the director and regulator of the people, and also responsible for

---

[33] K. Satchidananda Murty, *The Indian Spirit,* p. 94.

[34] Ibid., p. 96.

[35] Ibid., p. 222.

agriculture, economic prosperity, development and general welfare of the people. Kauṭilya's *Arthaśāstra* states that the king is not above the law. The Jātaka stories specify that a king is not the master of all citizens but of the law-breakers. The *Śukra-nīti* advocates that without any discussion with wise men, the king should not change the laws and conventions. These above-said ideals have been pragmatically existed in the ancient times. The Pāli Buddhist books recorded that there were republics governed by a body of kṣatriyas; and according to the accounts of Megasthenes, the Greek Ambassador of fourth century BC, there were republics like Licchavis of Vaiśālī, the Videhas of Mithilā, and Kathians of Sāṅkala. According to the *Mahābhārata*, Kṛṣṇa was the federal president over the confederation of the republics of the Yādavas, the Kakuras, and the Bhojas, though he particularly belonged to Sātvatas republic and though each republic had its own chief.[36]

The *Manusmṛti*, the Śāntiparva portion of the *Mahābhārata* and the *Arthaśāstra*, in general, advocated and idealized wars for establishing wide empires, occupying the neighbouring states. To become *Cakravartī* (emperor) for the whole land, lying in between the Himalayas and the South seas was the ideal for every Hindu king in ancient times. Some historians say that this idea led the Hindu kings to fight with the neighbouring kings; and thus India was never united, and which paved the way for successive invasions from outside India. Murty, in *Indian Spirit*, after a brief survey, reformulated the ancient Hindu politics and ethics to suit the present conditions. According to him, political actions represent the interest of either a leader or a group or a state. But in the field of diversity, opposition and historical confrontations, the action that oriented for "the common good is justified".[37]

---

[36] K. Satchidananda Murty, *The Indian Spirit*, pp. 223-25.

[37] Ibid., p. 233.

INDIAN HOSPITALITY AND UNIVERSALITY

Murty interprets that the Chinese tried to conquer, assimilate and absorb some aspects of other cultures into their "all-encompassing Chinese civilization"— the only civilization for them. While Westerners consider it as their duty to fight and overcome other cultures, the Indians never fought against any other culture. Murty says:

> . . . there is no religion and civilization other than the Hindu which took over so many elements from others. Countless foreigners — travellers, scholars and administrators — Greek, Chinese, Portuguese and British — have spoken about Indian hospitality and receptivity to men and ideas.[38]

Every nation whether Europe or India claims their rationality and spirituality is superior to those of others. The Jews and Christians believed that they have final revelation for salvation from the true and living God. But Murty, after critical observation, says that environment and tradition influence the human thinking and thereby the process of behaviour will go on. He writes:

> Whether in India, Europe, or Africa it is men who create culture and philosophies; and human nature is the same everywhere, for men have the same capacities, basic needs and aspirations all over the world.[39]

So many systems and dictums took shape in the annals of Indian mysticism, some are contradictory but nothing had shaken the culture of India. Spiritual consciousness is the driving force of global outlook. It is the cessation of once egoism, and has in its core, the thought of goodness and beauty. It makes one to perceive a single line of thought and

[38] K. Satchidananda Murty, *The Indian Spirit*, pp. 43-44.

[39] Ibid., p. 174.

action, where man identifies himself with the universe. It is the realization of whole world as one family, *vasudhaiva kuṭumbakam*. Murty concludes:

> Only then can our ancient Āryan ideal of *samatā sarvatra*, equality and equanimity everywhere, materialize. Then only can the kingdom of Heaven be ushered in.[40]

The spirit of Murty's argument is that the modern democratic state is always in tune with the consent of the majority. In ancient times much has happened, but the modern state being connected with the international sphere, has the global outlook. He writes:

> The impulses of man are slowly working towards the foundation of an international order which will create a civilized world in which human rights everywhere will be protected and poverty and war will be eliminated.[41]

Whatever the old methods and ideals of the individual state may be, the contemporary situation has created new interests, ideas, stirrings and impulses to secure an international order based on peace, justice and socio-economic equality. Therefore, Murty asserts the need for promotion of harmony, tolerance and universal ethics. He concludes that it is impossible to preach traditional morality without these values, as modern man is enlightened due to universal education and political awareness.

Murty says that Western scholars introduced most Indian classical literature and tradition with some bias in their psyche according to their understanding. As such it is not possible to comprehend the civilization of India in a fitting manner with alien psyche, but it should be rediscovered once again with an Indian mind.

---

[40] K. Satchidananda Murty, *Hinduism and Its Development*, p. 12.

[41] K. Satchidananda Murty, *The Indian Spirit*, p. 237.

5

Social Philosophy

THE study of social institutions is one of the aspects of social philosophy in which concepts and beliefs, values and ideals, basic issues of social relations both at national and international level have been undertaken. This is with reference to social unity of mankind, various aspects of social life and ideals spring from the circumstances of time and place; and they change and develop from age to age. Therefore the historical background has become the necessary base for understanding, and for the evolution of ideas in philosophy.

> History, which is occupied with the record of such circumstances and changes, throws light on many important aspects of social life; and, on the other hand, a general philosophy of society should help us to interpret what without it is apt to seem arbitrary and chaotic in the panorama of history.[1]

Murty in the same direction, probably influenced by either Hegel's philosophy of history or Bertrand Russell's interpretation of Western philosophy, has interpreted Indian philosophy with reference to social and political conditions. As early as in 1952 Murty wrote in his *Evolution of Philosophy in India* the need for presenting philosophy with reference to the socio-political conditions. He states:

---

1 J.S. Mackenzie, *Outlines of Social Philosophy*, p. 18.

> No thinker and philosophy can be considered in the abstract, they being the products of their social milieu. No historian of Indian philosophy has kept this fact in mind.[2]

Murty maintains that human ideals and values develop, not only with reference to the social conditions as basis but also in accordance with the psychological attitude of the individual who proposes them. Freud, the psychologist, says that the mind consists of two parts — the conscious and unconscious. Murty also accepts such modern theories and says:

> . . . the study of a man's character, of his habits and environment provides a clue towards understanding and appreciating his theories and beliefs. Not only is it necessary to study any theory in relation to the socio-economic structure in which it arises, but it is also necessary to pay attention to the character and personalities of the man who puts it forth.[3]

Finding out the social factors and geographical conditions as the basis for human speculations and beliefs has become one of the basic premises of Murty's philosophy. This is in accordance with Radhakrishnan's interpretation, which attributed the pessimistic perspective of Indian philosophy due to the geographical conditions prevailed in the north India. In his *Evolution of Philosophy in India* Murty points out that one's own social status or genetic leanings also influence one's way of thought. For example Buddha came from the tribe of Śākyas, who are kṣatriyas; in his dialogue he advocated the supremacy of kṣatriyas over brāhmaṇas. Actually Murty writes, Buddha had no kingdom; probably his father might be an

---

[2] K. Satchidananda Murty, *Evolution of Philosophy in India*, Preface, p. i.

[3] Ibid., p. 13.

elected leader of the neighbourhood; however in the later stories, Buddha was shown as a prince and his father a powerful monarch.[4]

Buddha, Murty writes, must have observed the social degradation of the traders, labourers and slaves and also the pitiable condition of women. The result was, after becoming an ascetic, Buddha criticized the claims of the brāhmaṇas. It is to be noted that Buddha neither tried to abolish the caste-system nor preached equality, but by criticizing the brāhmaṇas, he considered the kṣatriyas as "the best among Gods and men". Buddha remarked that a true brāhmaṇa is one who is virtuous and learned but not who is born in the brāhmaṇa caste.[5] Thus the brāhmaṇas have been criticized; and the supremacy of kṣatriyas was asserted. Similarly, Buddha applied the same measure to other castes, however, denied the caste-distinction among Buddhist monks.

Murty also traces the development of religious doctrines with the support of the people in power. The powerful and strong centralized government of Aśoka, after his embracement of Buddhism caused for the spread of Buddhism in the whole of India. Even in the modern times one witnesses the socio-political conditions as the cause for the propagation of certain ideologies. During the first forty years of independent India, Gandhian thought has been promoted, similar to the state nurture of "dialectical materialism" in the former Union of Soviet Socialist Republic (USSR) or Russia.

PHILOSOPHY OF INCLUSIVENESS

Murty has brought out the underlying factors of Indian

---

[4] K. Satchidananda Murty, *Evolution of Philosophy in India*, p. 112.

[5] Ibid., p. 124.

thought, which is a philosophy of inclusiveness.[6] His philosophical outlook stands for unity. According to him, though Hinduism is a religion based on Śrutis and Smṛtis, it has both theistic and atheistic elements. He writes:

> People who worship different gods, people who worship the same god in different ways, people who worship no god at all can all be Hindus.[7]

Probably the Hindu pluralism might be due to the absorption of different primitive tribes into the Hindu fold, which is also a method of inclusiveness. In other words different communities and people with various forms of worship and rituals, who were scattered throughout the country with diversities of blood, colour, language and manners, have formed into a people. Therefore Murty writes:

> Heterogeneous races, diverse ideas, multiple customs have all been welded together and a distinct culture, sublime and grandiose, has emerged.[8]

Murty has not limited his analysis to Hinduism but applied to the whole of Indian culture. Like every religious scripture that upholds values and principles, the culture of each country will have its own merits and demerits. According to Murty the person who has a deep understanding of his own culture will have also equal respect to other cultures. He concludes:

---

[6] R. Balasubrahmanian comments that Murty's method and scope of philosophy is that of inclusiveness. Vide his, "The Ramifications of the Real in the Philosophy of Inclusiveness" in Sibajiban Bhattacharyya and Ashok Vohra (eds.), *Philosophy of K. Satchidananda Murty*, p. 1.

[7] K. Satchidananda Murty, *Hinduism and Its Development*, p. 16.

[8] Ibid., p. 17.

> No culture, nation or religion can arrogate to itself the monopoly of either the revelation of God or person or of the experience of the impersonal absolute . . . God has many witnesses to all his truth both in the East and the West.[9]

There have been many books on Indian philosophy describing the six systems (*ṣaḍ-darśana*s) of Indian philosophy along with Jainism, Buddhism and Cārvākas, ignoring a number of sects and schools of ancient India, which have not been appropriately presented in Indian philosophy. This kind of pattern of writing the history of Indian philosophy was set forth first by Haribhadra and Mādhava, introduced in English by H.T. Colebrooke, followed by S.N. Dasgupta and Radhakrishnan. No doubt the doctrines and ideas expounded in these systems have influenced Indians down the ages, but it is also to be remembered that there have been individuals and schools who have equally influenced the people of India for centuries.

As a critique, Murty stands for the unity and understanding of all philosophies, and advocates the inclusion and study of the movements and schools of ancient India. He writes that the Tamil Saṅgam poetry stood for the egalitarian ideas, the Āḷvars and Nayanārs were primarily responsible for the Bhakti Movement. In the Middle Age a number of saints, *siddha*s and *guru*s have perpetuated glorious ideas which have influenced the Indian mind and life.[10] Thus, with his doctrine of inclusiveness, Murty advocates a harmonious Indian philosophy, wherein different thinkers of various streams of thought find their place appropriately. While writing books on contemporary Indian philosophy, he asks, why the writers did not include the philosophy of Narayana Guru, an Advaitin from Kerala who advocated oneness of humanity

---

[9] K. Satchidananda Murty, *The Indian Spirit*, p. 162.

[10] K. Satchidananda Murty, *Philosophy in India*, pp. 90-91.

on the basis of the great-sentences (*mahāvākyas*) of the Upaniṣads. Murty's book, *Indian Philosophy Since 1498* for the first time contains Ambedkar's views. It is to be noted that no other Indian philosopher has introduced the views and thoughts of Ambedkar to the Indian philosophic community so far. In this context, Murty's remarks are worth reading:

> For example, Narayana Guru, J. Krishnamurti, B.R. Ambedkar and some others are not in any way less important than many of those included in these textbooks, and some included deserved inclusion in more than one book.[11]

A number of books have been written on contemporary Indian philosophy by persons like S. Radhakrishnan, Margaret Chatterjee, N.K. Devaraj and others. But thinkers like Narayana Guru and Ambedkar, who have great following and admirers in the country and who have enriched the Indian thought, have not been included in those volumes, writes Murty.

SOCIAL DIALECTICS

Murty is a great applicant of "dialectical method" in his writings, which is evident from his narration of ideals and doctrines with social facts. There are certain striking remarks in his books on social contradictions; but a reader, who has not accustomed in the way Murty perceives, cannot absorb immediately, the reason for the assertions he made. Both in his earlier and later writings, starting from *Evolution of Philosophy in India* to the *Philosophy in India,* Murty maintained the dialectical method of presenting the contradictions involved while narrating principles, ideals, and notions of social and metaphysical importance. When the great philosophical writers — Russell and Radhakrishnan — presented the social,

[11] K. Satchidananda Murty, *Philosophy in India,* p. 101.

economic conditions for the rise of ideas and schools, Murty brings out the forgotten factor of individual instincts and psychological reasons. When the modern followers of Buddha praise him as the champion of equality and eradicator of caste, Murty mentions that there is no evidence in the Buddhist literature that Buddha tried to abolish caste as a social institution. He also points out that Buddha has asserted the superiority of kṣatriyas over the brāhmaṇas stating the former as a first caste of the *varṇa-vyavasthā*.

Books on Indian philosophy or Hindu thought or Hinduism necessarily describe, in general, in their earlier chapters about the fourfold caste system. As per the order of castes mentioned in the Puruṣa-Sūkta of the *R̥gveda* and some of the Smr̥ti literature — like the *Manusmr̥ti* and the *Bhagavad-Gītā,* it is said that the duty of the brāhmaṇas is the study of the Vedas. But Murty, while admitting the superiority of the brāhmaṇas as described in those books, brings out the fact that they are the people officiating marriages and death ceremonies, and also medical men. In the Upaniṣads, the brāhmaṇas and the kṣatriyas were mentioned as the seekers of the *Brahman*-knowledge and learned from each other about the Ultimate Reality. In this context, Murty brings out the Upaniṣadic story about the man called Raikva, who lived outside the village in a cart, probably a gipsy, and but has been considered as a great teacher. The four-fold caste system, which was described in the Śrutis and Smr̥tis, was never a fact in the society in the strict sense of the term. It is worth mentioning what Murty writes:

> While the Gr̥hya-Sūtras and Smr̥tis described the four castes and four life stages, one can justifiably wonder whether this scheme was ever anything more than a norm of social organization held up before people. One wonders whether the brāhmaṇas ever held the position

> which these books held, i.e. as the guides, preceptors and mentors of kings and of great merchant princes. The Ithihāsas and the Purāṇas, if carefully and critically read, do not show any evidence of brāhmaṇa domination in secular matters. Some brāhmaṇa priests may have traded on people's superstitions and at times may have tyrannized society by acting as provocative agents and by fomenting factions and political troubles and finding themselves in the victorious camp as advisers and guides.[12]

Ideals that were never in practice, but described in books and in circulation as ideals, have been discussed in the *Indian Spirit* contrary to the popular belief. In other words, books written by Indologists or authors interested in Indian culture and heritage contain the idealistic view of life with reference to the four *varṇa*s, four *āśrama*s and four *puruṣārtha*s as described in the Hindu scriptures (Dharmaśāstras). Murty remarks that in actuality there is no historical evidence that they having been practised.

This kind of theoretical perspective, though mentioned in some Hindu Dharmaśāstras, Murty writes, was never a fact even in the scripture. For example, the *Ṛgveda,* which describes the four *varṇa*s and compares them with the four parts of the *puruṣa,* does mention a number of other professionals and artisans in different places. The point to be noted is that Murty is not against either to any caste or scripture but wants to realize the facts of the scriptures and the society. When greatness is attributed to a particular caste, while the others are downgraded, Murty sees the contradiction and points out the nobility of the inferior. When a kind of thesis is maintained, asserted and advocated there should also be a need to know the antithesis, which paves the way to the synthesis or

[12] K. Satchidananda Murty, *The Indian Spirit,* p. 13.

Absolute Truth. The Absolute Truth is known when subjective truth and objective truth are synthesized. Murty is not interested in knowing one side of the truth; for him Indian society is a harmonious mosaic of various castes or communities; and a unity has to be maintained in thought, like in reality. However there have been certain lacunas; and one need not be proud of one's own heritage. In this context Bhauvan Chandel remarks about Murty:

> The injustice and irrationality of the caste system as it was and is, has been condemned by Murty whenever he had to write about Hindu society.[13]

Murty also examined certain theories associated with the origin of caste system in India on the basis of scriptures. The *Bhagavad-Gītā* says that the division of castes is due to the character (*guṇa*) and profession (*karma*); it also explains that God is the creator of the castes. But a number of brāhmanical books of ancient India also mentioned the occupational changes. Except the priesthood, which is the prerogative of the brāhmaṇas, all other professions have been adopted by different castes. For example, commerce and agriculture were open to all castes. Leaving aside these doctrines entertained by the Hindu scriptures about the origin of the caste system, Murty has brought out and discussed the racial elements for the origin of caste system on the basis of the migration and arrival of different groups and races to India.

Murty has a liberal and moderate outlook about caste system in India. He writes that the caste system is not intended to perpetuate inequalities and fascist tendencies; it is a kind of social arrangement to accommodate different racial types, and a solution for the problem of racial conflict fought out by

[13] Sibajiban Bhattacharyya and Ashok Vohra (eds.), op. cit., p. 289.

the Āryans. He declined to accept the caste system as the creation of the wicked priests. The Āryans did not kill the people they conquered like the victorious white man, who massacred the Red Indians in the US, the Bushmen of the Pacific Island and the tribals of Australia, but invented a method of assimilation and reform. The Āryan sects kept aloof from themselves; and the aboriginal races were not asked to surrender their individuality. Sometimes some tribes were allowed into their fold. For example, the Rājpūts of the royal races, who were originally the Turcoman tribes of Central Asia, have been admitted into the Hindu fold.

The fundamental point associated with the caste system is that different races that arrived in India had kept their identity and have not killed the conquered people, but kept them as a separate group that resulted in different castes. Referring to the evolution of castes from races, Murty writes:

> Each one of these exclusive groups, representing a distinct type, formed a different caste and as time moved on, the number of castes began to increase with the increase in the number of races absorbed. But there was no oppression of one caste by another. Each realized that it was but an individual unit of the harmonious whole.[14]

Though there have been a number of interpretations about caste system both classical and modern, Murty's interpretation is close to the discoveries in anthropology about Indian society. It has also been said that India is a museum of races. There have been the elements of Negroid races in the south and Mongoloid elements in the north, while the elements related to the people of East-European races are found in the

---

[14] K. Satchidananda Murty, *Hinduism and Its Development*, pp. 65-66.

northwest and Mongoloid elements in the north-east of India. Thus those people who arrived in India subsequently interacted with the local people or groups. The caste that originated became mutually complementary but not contradictory, and the mixture of different groups was discouraged, though transgressors were there.

The conclusion is that Murty's analysis of caste system paves the way to differentiate the doctrines written in the Brāhmanical books or Sanskrit literature on one hand and the real facts of anthropological discoveries that were there in the society on the other hand. While the books of ancient times describe a kind of ideal theory, Murty brings out the visible facts of the social structure in the society. He is really a social critique, writing and advocating the fact and bringing out the truth by studying the classical scriptures (Śāstras) in the contemporary times. In this context, Sengaku Mayeda writes:

> Murty is a rare Indian philosopher who has paid much attention to the socio-political setting of modern or contemporary Indian philosophy.[15]

PHILOSOPHY FOR SOCIETY

Whether one calls it a Marxist point or Russellian interpretation, Murty from his early writings onwards, from his *Evolution of Philosophy in India* (1952), until *Indian Philosophy Since 1498* (1982), has discussed philosophy in relation to social and political circumstances, and physical and geographical conditions as causes. He says:

> . . . new conceptions and beliefs have been formulated in every age to be discarded, modified, confirmed, or

---

[15] Sibajiban Bhattacharyya and Ashok Vohra (eds.), op. cit. p. 124.

> developed in the same or succeeding ages. All these, however, do not arise in a vacuum, but in a particular *milieu*. Social and political circumstances as well as legal and other institutions influence their origins, shaping and growth. Economic necessities and development condition and mould politics and social institutions, whereas political and social theories, views and institutions, in their turn, influence economic development.[16]

The religious and philosophical ideas, which were the products of their time, again react upon the whole development of the society. Therefore Murty says that philosophy should be used as a transforming agent in a stagnant society. His philosophy is used to inculcate the students the habit of reflecting upon the prevailing thought and issues of their time that may positively contribute to the development of society. Murty reminds about the 1953 Unesco report, which asserts the inclusion of actual experience, the data of modern science, the significance of arts and culture, social and moral problems in the syllabi of philosophy:

> . . . philosophical problems are simply the problems of life itself, dealt within a lucid and coherent manner and clarified by the thinking of the great philosophers of the past. It is the task of teachers to bring out the human interest of the teaching of philosophy.[17]

S. Radhakrishnan, apart from his classical learning and writing, wrote about the issues of civilization, human progress, poverty and social reconstruction. P.T. Raju asserted that philosophy should be made socially useful. D.P. Chattopadhyaya has expounded the idea of Indian philosophical heritage for social

---

[16] K. Satchidananda Murty, *Indian Philosophy Since 1498*, p. 20.

[17] K. Satchidananda Murty, *Philosophy in India*, p. 174.

progress. A number of prominent philosophy professors like S.S. Barlingay, Rajendra Prasad, Daya Krishna and K.J. Shaw have contributed much on political, social and moral philosophy. Any teacher, who is committed for metaphysical, epistemological issues of philosophy, is definitely doing valuable service, but the social issues should also be taken. Murty says:

> Those who are completely engaged in ontology, metaphysics, analysis or formal logic or history of philosophy are doing equally valuable work. But there seems to be a moral and professional obligation on the part of a philosopher to conduct his inquiries relating to religious, moral, social and political matters.[18]

He says that philosophers and other social scientists could do much in such a way inspiring people to become altruistic and moral. He writes:

> Academic men including philosophers could do much in this direction by strengthening the moral motivation of people by, first of all, leading their personal lives in a such a way that morality becomes "fashionable", which it is not today, and then by developing contemporaneously relevant normative ethics through uni-disciplinary as well as multi-disciplinary studies undertaken singly and jointly.[19]

[18] K. Satchidananda Murty, *Philosophy in India*, p. 176.

[19] Ibid., p. 183.

Conclusion

PROF. Murty is a unique philosopher of international repute, grounded in Indian culture as well as well-versed in the philosophies of the East and West, interpreting Indian philosophy in the context of social, political and geographical conditions. According to him, philosophy stands for the evolution of all ideas with reference to religious, political, social and educational aspects of human life; it is the critique of ideologies and the rational examination of the foundation of belief and faith.

Murty belongs to a guild of philosophical community that inculcates the wisdom of the philosophies of different nations, studying and imbibing the major areas of philosophy. He served for forty years as philosophy teacher, wrote and published books in a span of fifty-five years.

During his active and academic life, Murty had attained the highest state honours. He was chosen for the best positions of the philosophical associations and addressed the major philosophical conferences held in different universities. He was committed in word and deed to international understanding and development of philosophy in India. The editors of the book, *Philosophy of K. Satchidananda Murty* aptly put forward how he impressed the people known to him.

> Those who have the privilege of knowing Murty personally know that besides being a profound scholar, a distinguished teacher and an efficient and able administrator, he has many endearing personal qualities. As we consider it to be our

> privilege to be among his friends, we resist the temptation to use our editorial prerogative to discuss his personality.[1]

Though he became a great scholar, in the later part of his life, being trained in many languages in childhood, he proved himself a prodigy by writing a commentary in Telugu on the *Bhagavad-Gītā* at the age of thirteen.

SCIENTIFIC ANALYSIS OF HINDUISM

Murty was trained in the fundamentals and principles of Hindu Dharmaśāstras and the philosophy of Vedānta. He stood for the evolution of Hinduism and scientific analysis and assessment of the origin of caste system different from the accepted Hindu Dharmaśāstra view of life, which differs from the actual social structure of the Indian villages. Murty proposed the right evaluation of the Hindu scriptures being the student of Sanskrit and believer of Hindu religion. He writes:

> While none can have greater regard and love for Indian culture and the Indian way of life than myself, I am for viewing things objectively and scientifically, unclogged by misplaced patriotism and love for the past.[2]

Murty, after retirement, had invited the Śaṅkarācārya of Śṛṅgerī to his native place, Saṅgam Jagarlamudi and felicitated him with golden flowers poured on his head; and the Śaṅkarācārya gave *darśana* and benisons to the dignitaries and members attended on that occasion.[3]

---

[1] Sibajivan Bhattacharyya and Ashok Vohra (eds.), *The Philosophy of K. Satchidananda Murty*, Preface, p. ix.

[2] K. Satchidananda Murty, *Evolution of Philosophy in India*, Preface, p. i.

[3] Veeramachaneni Sangameswara Rao has informed me that the arrival of Śaṅkarācārya of Śṛṅgerī in Sangam Jagarlamudi.

Hinduism as a religion consists of theists and atheists, sceptics and agnostics, worshippers of nature and believers of supernatural divine beings, followers of sacrifices and adherents of theological pursuits. Therefore, Murty remarks that Hinduism is supratheistic based upon experience. He believes and asserts that the Hindu scriptures have to be understood rightly and be interpreted taking into consideration all issues and aspects as a whole. He asserts that presentation of particular beliefs and ideals favourable to us is not the right way of interpreting the ancient scriptures.

While studying the Vedas or the Upaniṣads, Murty argues that there is a need to note down accurately the facts, however they may be small, along with the narration of ideals. Whenever there are conglomeration of facts and ideals and the understanding of things comprehensively, there is every possibility of knowing the truth and the application of it in a possible right direction. He writes in his *Revelation and Reason in Advaita Vedānta:*

> I did not devote any space to the "higher criticism" of the Vedas. A perusal of this book will reveal that I am not a Hindu fundamentalist. I hold that the principles and the methodology that had been evolved in the West since the time of Spinoza's *Tractatus* for interpreting the Bible ought to be applied to all religious scriptures. The various points I make in the last part of this book make it clear that Vedic studies would result in sound conclusion only when the higher criticism of the texts is not neglected.[4]

MADHYAMIKA: COMPARATIVE PHILOSOPHY

Murty, in the beginning as a young scholar, was an

---

[4] K. Satchidananda Murty, *Revelation and Reason in Advaita Vedānta*, Preface, pp. x-xi.

independent thinker, he studied the classics and inferred the conclusions, however there seem to be assertions without explanations. The treatment of the subject with which he goes on writing may not seem to be convincing for those readers who are interested in elaborate discussions for pages together. But Murty assembles dialectically the relevant ideas and facts one by one that can give us the real meaning that he wanted to convey. He projects his own reflections deliberately and drastically based upon the sourcebooks and classical literature. In the earlier writings of Murty, verses and ideals of classical literature along with facts and figures have been juxtaposed to present the truth. Later, he changed the methodology; advocated his views through presenting the remarks and points expressed by others. He narrated similar views and contradictory statements taking from the philosophies of East and West, quoting the classical and modern interpretations, in order to lead towards the conclusion. Sometimes he seemed to be a Buddhist Mādhyamika, not advocating Nihilism but presenting the facts without arriving at a conclusion. In other words he presented different standpoints, contradictory statements both positive and negative. Therefore it was highly impossible to find out what Murty was telling about; in this context a remark made by N. Isayeva may be cited:

> While Murty himself was much too modest insisting that nowhere in his book *Revelation and Reason in Advaita Vedānta* were the personal views of the author explicitly expressed, in my opinion, the author's position is only too clear to the attentive reader, though, of course, it was intricately interwoven into the texture of the monograph.[5]

Murty could be considered as a comparative philosopher as

---

[5] N. Isayeva, "Sitting at the Feet of Śaṅkara" in Sibajivan Bhattacharyya and Ashok Vohra (eds.), op. cit., p. 149.

he adopted the comparative method. Comparative philosophy is a new field of study adopted from the comparative methodology of theology. As there were books on comparative religion and comparative theology for a long time, the same comparative method has been extended to the field of philosophy applying comparison on the problems, attitudes, methods, activities, conclusions and effects.[6]

Comparative philosophy proceeds with a positive outlook and human interest. It is a comprehensive outlook that tries to synthesize two aspects on a point by avoiding one-sidedness of a philosophical approach. A comparative philosopher of one civilization must try to understand the civilization of others by exploring differences and similarities. While discussing a problem certain generalizations have to be arrived on the basis of examples and evidences; and complementary characters and interconnectedness may be discovered. By discovering significant differences or similarities, the comparative philosopher arrives at certain judgement, which helps for global understanding. In the same spirit, S. Radhakrishnan had aptly presented the Indian philosophy to the Western world by comparing the theological statements and philosophical explanations while explaining the schools of Indian philosophy. According to P.T. Raju comparative philosophy may "ought to lead to such a system which will be inclusive of both the Eastern and Western outlooks".[7]

Comparative philosophy shows the relation of a thinker's philosophy to his environment, sometimes in another tradition too. This kind of studies many a time may be sociological or historical; but implications will be drawn keeping in view the nature of man for integral outlook. Accordingly Raju writes:

---

[6] Archie J. Bahm, *Comparative Philosophy*, p. 6.

[7] P.T. Raju, *Lectures on Comparative Philosophy*, p. 7.

> . . . comparative philosophy cannot be mere phenomenology, although it studies philosophies as phenomena appearing in different cultural areas. It has also to point out how far the different philosophies and their traditions have succeeded in elucidating the nature of man and the universe. The aim thus is a kind of humanism, but a humanism that is critico-integral, critical in the sense that it critically evaluates the different philosophies and traditions so far as their understanding of human nature is concerned.[8]

While describing the impact of Buddhism on society, as early as in his *Hinduism and Its Development,* Murty discussed the social perspective of Buddha's teaching that "all men belong to one *saṁgha,* they should live together and lead a common life of righteousness". In this context, he says that the Buddhist doctrine of equality and love, establishment of new social order and condemnation of all private wealth anticipates a pattern of society, similar to Marxian materialism and Gandhian idealism. In his *The Realm of Between* Murty maintained the comparative method, while discussing the doctrine of suffering in Buddhism drawing similarities with that of Christian theology and philosophies of German thinkers. His books — *The Quest for Peace; The Indian Spirit; Metaphysics, Man and Freedom* and *Far Eastern Philosophies* — contained numerous comparisons while discussing different ideas, notions and doctrines. In this context, N.S.S. Raman remarks:

> Murty should be regarded as one of the pioneers of comparative philosophy (along with Radhakrishnan and P.T. Raju) in this country. He applies the comparative method more systematically and rigorously than Radhakrishnan. Rich tributes have already been paid to his profound and deep

[8] P.T. Raju, *Lectures on Comparative Philosophy,* p. 9.

scholarship of the various philosophical traditions of the world.[9]

PHILOSOPHY AS ĀṆVIKṢIKĪ

Philosophy and religion are different from each other; though some of the topics are same, the interpretations are different. Religion is based upon tradition, authority, classical texts, faith and rituals, whereas philosophy stands for reason, individual analysis and logical conclusions. Murty asserts that philosophy is a systematic knowledge that arises out of human thought, not based upon belief and scriptures but provides new ideas, new possible ways of looking at things and also the possible way to evaluate them. Quits and creeds, ideologies and hopes are not philosophy for him, hence defines philosophy:

> . . . Philosophy is the critique of ideologies and also the rational examination and evolution of the foundations of belief and faith.[10]

Murty agrees with Max Müller that there is little philosophy in Pūrva-Mīmāṁsā. For him, though there are similarities between Indian philosophy and Western philosophy, Indian philosophy is more close to scholastic philosophy, which was neglected in Indian universities. He writes that the chief aim and characteristic of both scholasticism and Indian philosophy are to systematize and rationalize religious dogmas. He remarks that the history of Indian philosophy has ignored criticism, while in Europe philosophy with its new outlook in methodology has departed from theology. But in India, according to him, Bruno

---

[9] N.S.S. Raman, "Comparative Method in Philosophy and Religion" in Sibajiban Bhattacharyya and Ashok Vohra (eds.), op. cit., p. 209.

[10] K. Satchidananda Murty, *Philosophy in India*, p. 178.

and Descartes are yet to born. Except Lokāyata and Sāṁkhya, we do not have any Indian philosophy exclusively based on reason. Therefore Murty advocates that we should extract philosophy from theological texts or the Vedic scriptures. Hence, he says:

> We do not find any clear distinction between philosophy and theology, reason and faith as is found in Thomas Aquinas. . . . In the case of all the schools it is possible to some extent to extract their philosophy from their concomitant theological and mythological trappings, and assess the value of such philosophy. Only then can a history of Indian philosophy be accomplished, which, it can be asserted, is no light task.[11]

Though in the conventional sense, Murty accepts Indian philosophy as *darśana,* he prefers *Āṇvikṣikī* as an appropriate term to indicate philosophy, as its meaning is "the science of systematic investigation and logical demonstration", that reflects the real goal of philosophy. He has been an advocate of reorganization of Indian philosophy with a retrospective perspective. He believes that there should be difference between religion and philosophy, and points out that the histories of Indian philosophy failed to distinguish between religion and philosophy. Therefore he asserts:

> Philosophy is the search of the intellect for truth, while religion is the cry of the heart for salvation. . . . The point of departure for a history of philosophy is the distinction between philosophy and religion.[12]

The concept of philosophy — the theme and content — is an issue for Murty to ponder over. He is of the opinion that there is no uniformity on the concept of philosophy in India: for

[11] K. Satchidananda Murty, *Evolution of Philosophy in India,* p. 51.

[12] Ibid., Preface, p. i.

some people it is *brahma-vidyā* or *ātma-vidyā,* for Vedic scholars it is *brahmodaya,* for Buddhists it is *dṛṣṭi* or *prajñā.* According to the *Bhagavad-Gītā* it is the *ādhyātmika-vidyā* or *tattva-jñāna,* and for Kauṭilya it is *Āṇvikṣikī.* But the ancient Indian writers named their volumes on philosophy as *darśana*s.

Murty in his later writing, *Philosophy in India,* which discusses the tradition, teaching and research of philosophy in India raises the meaning and role of philosophy and does arrive at the importance of philosophical diversity in India. However, he proposes that there is a need to construct Indian philosophy on the basis of the geographical, social and political conditions and point of view. For him, not only the Indian classical texts but also the modern and contemporary writings did not contain philosophy based on and with reference to the social and political and living issues of life. Therefore Murty asserts that an Indian philosopher has to concern himself with the non-religious and socio-political thinking while analysing Indian philosophy.

INESCAPABLE METAPHYSICAL THINKING

The unique nature of human being is, not only to concern himself with the day-to-day problems and visible things but also invisible things and the life beyond. For Plato, philosophers are those people "who are able to grasp that which is always invariable and unchanging".[13] Not only philosophers but even simple thinking human beings, due to dependency, despair, suffering, tragic (or) death force to think, make to relate the causes of the effects and events, try to find out the unforeseen mover, unforeseen element, unmoved mover and the mysterious being. Though one tries to

[13] Cf. K. Satchidananda Murty, *An Exercise in Mystical Ontology,* Presidential Address of the Akhila Bharatiya Darshan Parishad, Ninth Session, Lucknow University, 3 October 1963, p. 1.

understand it, but could not grasp it. Thus the search for the cause, the hope for refugee and the solution for the perplexity constitute the transcendent. Murty writes:

> The transcendent is mysterious, for although it is already around us, enmeshing us, involving us in itself, interpenetrating us and encompassing us; its nature is not comprehended by us, for it is not given to us, not present to us as a datum.[14]

Human contemplation and the transcendent, though difficult and rare, there are people who think about the mystery of the world, which consistently lead to know the unknown. While human suffering and sin, despair and death, failure and anguish, finitude and flux speak the limitations of man outwardly, and whenever they grip the soul, man also thinks inwardly the other way towards the eternal, infinite, delight and the boundless. Thus metaphysics arises, which is the intellectual, psychological and linguistic human endeavour. Murty says that man, as reflective being does need a metaphysical view; even those who are opposed to metaphysics find metaphysical thinking inescapable. Similarly, man has to be born in a particular tradition, which is prior to him. Though one transcends one's tradition and adept another tradition but cannot be without tradition. Murty writes: "To escape tradition completely is to annihilate oneself. . . ."[15]

Murty departs from the dualism of self and body, which attaches sins to the body and freedom to the self. He says that it is impossible for man in the world to escape from the laws of the nature and remain as a man who does not attach to the world, in which we live and enjoy. Therefore, for him, freedom from the world consists in accepting the real position

[14] Cf. K. Satchidananda Murty, *An Exercise in Mystical Ontology*, p. 3.

[15] K. Satchidananda Murty, *Metaphysics, Man and Freedom*, p. 53.

in the world aspiring for the awareness of the transcendent or the Divine Being. Murty asserts that man is real, the world is real, and his participation in the world and history is real; but freedom consists of the responsible behaviour by realizing his relation to the transcendent or the Divine Being, the knowledge of which is freedom.

PHILOSOPHY OF INCLUSIVENESS

The method of Murty is the philosophy of inclusiveness, and he asserts that human nature is same everywhere. The comparative method adopted by him implies the fact that it has the basic prerequisite of interconnectedness of scattered fragments of diverse systems in other philosophies, cultures and civilizations. A person, who can perceive and have the knowledge of other philosophies, values, ideals and concepts can compare what presupposes the instinct of inclusiveness.

The philosophy of inclusiveness is nothing but a comprehensive understanding of not only the major areas of philosophies in the East and West but also advancing an integrated approach of dealing the whole aspects of philosophy. The remark made by R. Balasubramanian on the philosophy of Murty[16] is as follows:

> An outstanding Indian philosopher whose writings are remarkable as much for their width as for their depth is Radhakrishnan. Murty follows the lead and direction provided by this galaxy of philosophical luminaries of the East and the West belonging to classical, modern, and contemporary times.

The "inclusiveness" in the philosophy of Murty is a kind of global perspective and a method of synthesis for universal

[16] R. Balasubrahmanian, "The Ramfications of the Real in the Philosophy of Inclusiveness" in Sibajiban Bhattacharyya and Ashok Vohra (eds)., op. cit., p. 3.

understanding. While discussing the concept of Indian philosophy the authors generally refer to the meaning of either *darśana* or *tattva-jñāna;* but Murty's narration of different words and terms used in various texts of different systems of Indian philosophy reveals his approach of inclusiveness.

According to Murty, the history of Indian philosophy should not be limited to the study of the *ṣaḍ-darśana*s, the two religions and the Cārvākas but should also include religions and philosophical movements spread over the whole of India, from Kanyakumari to Kashmir. A study of the north Indian saints and *guru*s is as much important as that of the philosophers of south India. The other striking aspect of Murty's doctrine of inclusiveness is with reference to contemporary philosophy. A number of books devoted to contemporary philosophy have neither adopted any standard nor included every thinker. Not only the medieval thinkers like Tukārām, Rāmadās, Vemana, Sarvajñātma and Jñāneśwar were ignored but also Narayana Guru, Swami Ramatirtha, Muhammed Iqbal, Mahatma Gandhi and Ambedkar have been neglected. Therefore he says that the history of Indian philosophy should include the philosophy that developed in all periods of Indian history, in all regional languages and in all religions.

With reference to the content of each system of Indian philosophy, Murty says that the authors have emphasized a lot on metaphysics, epistemology and ethics, neglecting or minimizing the social and political aspects of philosophy. Even the writers of philosophy in recent years have not been careful about the contributions made by philosophers with reference to social and political realities. In this historical context, Murty reminds the great influence of Plato's *Republic* and the tremendous impact of Locke's *Two Treatises on Government.* Therefore in his works and thought Murty stressed for the evolution of Indian philosophy in relation to its social, political and geographical background.

The authors of the histories of philosophy in the West have limited their studies to Western philosophy only, forgetting the contributions made by the Indians and Chinese. According to them philosophy is that which aroused in Greece and inculcated in the universities of Europe or West. In this context, Murty says that philosophy should neither be limited to a country nor a nation, language and culture, as there is neither Western physics nor Indian physics. Similarly philosophy should not be identified with a particular nation or country, for the world is larger than the West. The Western and Indian philosophical thoughts do not absorb the philosophical world, just as they do not fill the whole world. But Murty advocates a global perspective of philosophy. He further insists the understanding of the philosophies of Far East, and says as follows:

> Most of our philosophy departments do not seem to know that the Chinese too have got a philosophical heritage as old, rich and continuous as that of the West and India, that the Muslim world produced thinkers (Ibn Sina, Al-Ghazzali, Ibn Rushd and Ibn Khaldun) second to none, and that modern East Asia has produced thinkers like Fung-Yu-lan and Kitaro Nishida who are in no way inferior to the best philosophers of the West or India.[17]

When the philosophy departments in Indian universities have swept away by teaching the Western philosophies, as head of the philosophy committees while drafting the curriculum, Murty pioneered the introduction and study of Chinese and Japanese philosophies. His *Far Eastern Philosophies* is an ample evidence for his commitment for global understanding, in his

[17] K. Satchidananda Murty, *Philosophy in India,* p. 202.

career as researcher. Of its importance in the philosophical knowledge, "dialectical materialism" as specialization was taught for more than two decades in Andhra University.

Murty did not advocate either to construct or to evolve a world philosophy. When the six systems (*ṣaḍ-darśana*s) of Indian philosophy were not synthesized into a single unified system, Murty asks, how could it be possible to evolve a world philosophy, inclusive of all the Indian and non-Indian philosophies? On the other hand, Murty argues that an ideal philosophy is that which is globally informed, open to the multiple traditions. His motto is "global understanding with Vedāntic spirit" deriving from the great sentence of the Upaniṣads, "that art thou" (*tat tvam asi*). In this context, the contribution made by Murty is well commented by Stephen H. Phillips:

> To my mind, one of the greatest challenges facing philosophers today — perhaps the greatest challenge — is a new globalism, the forging of a sense of a world history of philosophy and the making of an integrative response to the individual traditions of the past. With respect to this task, K. Satchidananda Murty is a leader, a path finder who has insisted on globality in the study of philosophy and has created an attractive integrative response in his own asserted views.[18]

A GREAT SOCIAL PHILOSOPHER

Murty is a great Indian philosopher of contemporary times, in the sense that no other philosopher made such a radical interpretation as he has done of Hindu scriptures with reference to social and political philosophy, except Swami

---

[18] Stephen H. Phillips, "The Ideal of Philosophy as Globally Informed" in Sibajiban Bhattacharyya and Ashok Vohra (eds.), op. cit., pp. 110-11.

Vivekananda and M.N. Roy. Murty outlined the evolution of Indian philosophy with reference to the social, political conditions, and also advocated for the teaching of philosophy with reference to the concrete reality and current problems. He writes:

> Those who are completely engaged in ontology, metaphysics, analysis or formal logic, or history of philosophy are doing equally valuable work. But there seems to be a moral and professional obligation on the part of a philosopher to conduct his enquiries relating to religious, moral, social and political matters."[19]

Murty says that it would be good if a considerable number of philosophy teachers concern themselves to discuss and evaluate all philosophical ideas in relation to legal, political, social and educational aspects.

Murty is a great social philosopher of contemporary India, who has interpreted the social implication of the metaphysics of Vedānta. On the basis of the great sentences (*mahāvākyas*) of the Upaniṣads, Vivekananda had advocated the equality of all human beings as the creator of the world and beings, *Brahman* lives in all beings. Murty further interprets that caste and occupation were not the criteria for *brahma-vidyā* for that in the *Brahma-sūtra-bhāṣya,* Śaṅkara has prescribed the four pre-requisites (*sādhana-catuṣṭaya*) for learning *Brahman*-knowledge. This may be substantiated with the story mentioned in Śaṅkara's biography about the untouchable, who questions Śaṅkara when the same *brahman* lives in all bodies according to Advaita, why there should be a difference?

On 16 September 1985 Murty addressed before the present Śaṅkarācārya of Śṛṅgerī, Sri Bharatitirtha Swami and said that the ethical and socio-political implications of transcendental

[19] K. Satchidananda Murty, *Philosophy in India,* p. 176.

knowledge of Advaita Vedānta are also important. Murty affirms that as the true self is devoid of castes and life stages, the true awareness is beyond those conceptions. He states:

> The consequence of the awareness of identity necessarily results in equality. The metaphysics of Advaita can be the foundation only for unselfishness and altruism and is consistent only with an egalitarian society based on social and economic justice, equality and peace.[20]

Thus, at the core of his heart, Murty is the most radical social philosopher of India, for he has pioneered the study and interpretation of Advaita Vedānta and Indian philosophy contrary to the accepted traditional beliefs on the basis of Vedic scriptures.

[20] K. Satchidananda Murty, *The Advaitic Notion,* p. 43.

Appendix I

Profile of K. Satchidananda Murty

Birth	25 September 1924
Father	Kotta Veerabhadraiah
Mother	Rajaratnamma
Wife	Vedavati Devi
Native Place	Sangam Jagarlamudi Via: Tenali, Guntur District Andhra Pradesh
Death	24 January 2011

Posts Held

1946-47	Lecturer in Philosophy, S.V. College, Tirupati
Aug.-Oct. 1948	Professor of Logic, M.P.C. College, Mayurbhanj, Orissa.
July 1949	Joined as Lecturer in Philosophy, Andhra University
1954-67	Head, Department of Philosophy, Andhra University
1967-71	Principal and Special Officer, Andhra University Post-graduate Centre, Guntur

1971-73	Head, Department of Philosophy, Andhra University
1960-84	Professor of Philosophy, Andhra University
1975-78	Vice-chancellor, S.V. University, Tirupati
1986-89	Vice-chairman, University Grants Commission, New Delhi

HONOURS

1963	General President, Akhila Bharatiya Darshan Parishad, Ninth Session, Lucknow University
1966-69	University Orator
1968	General President, Indian Philosophical Congress, Patna University
1980	Chairman, Indian Philosophical Congress

DEGREES AND ASSIGNMENTS

1980	Honorary D.Litt., Sampurnanand Sanskrit Vishwavidyalaya, Varanasi
1982	D.Litt., Andhra University, Waltair
1983	D.Litt., Nagarjuna University, Guntur
1985	D.Litt., S.V. University, Tirupati
1959	Visiting Professor (taught for a term), Princeton University
1963	Spalding lectures
1970	Visiting Professor, Indian Institute of Advanced Studies, Simla
1973-75	National Fellow (UGC)
1978	National Lecturer (UGC) in Philosophy

AWARDS

1980	A.P. State Award for Meritorious Teachers
1982	Dr. B.C. Roy National Award
1982	Raja Lakshmi Foundation Award
1983	Swami Pranavananda Philosophy National Award
1984	Padmabhushan Award (Govt. of India)
1984-86	National Fellow, Indian Council of Philosophical Research.
2001	Padmavibhushan Award (Govt. of India)

EXTENSION LECTURES DELIVERED

1954	University of Cairo
1956	University of Chicago and University of Wisconsin
1959	University of Columbia
1959	Universities of Goettingen, Mainz, Marburg and Bologna
1960	University of Annamalai
1962	University of Rajasthan
1963	University of Peshawar
1963	Universities of Tehran, Ankara, Oxford, Cambridge and London
1966	Philosophy Club, California and University of Mysore
1979	Bangalore University
1980	Utkal University

1981	Central Institute of Higher Tibetan Studies, Sarnath, Varanasi
1982	Beijing and Hong Kong
1984	Nepal

DISTINGUISHED TALKS

1977	Sri Aurobindo Memorial Lecture, Burdwan University
1978	Motilal Memorial Lectures, Hyderabad
1980	Preinnath Memorial Lecture, Punjab University
1980	Radhakrishnan Memorial Lecture, Telugu Academy
1980	Convocation Address, Sampurnanand Sanskrit Vishwavidyalaya, Varanasi
1980	Miller Lecture, Madras University
1980	K.B. Iyer Endowment Lecture, The Sanskrit Academy, Madras
1980	Pal Lectures, Calcutta University
1980	Debendranath Tagore Lecture, Viswabharati
1981	Founder's Day Lecture, Bhandarkar Oriental Research Institute, Poona
1982	Swami Vivekananda Memorial Lectures, Calcutta University
1983	Endowment Lectures on Vedanta, S.V. University, Tirupati
1984	L.M.J. Memorial Lecture on Buddhism, Tibetan Institute, Sarnath

1984	All India Oriental Conference Memorial Lectures, Karnataka University
1984	Lecture on Buddhism under the Auspices of Central Monastic Council, Thimphu, Bhutan

CONFERENCES ATTENDED

1959	Conference on Non-Alignment, Princeton University
1959	Conference on Religion and Freedom, Dallas, U.S.A.
1965	Conference on Inter-Religious Problems, Princeton
1975	Inter-Religious Peace Colloquium, Bellagio, Italy
1976	Vice-chancellors Conference, New Zealand
1976	Presided over a Session of the International Congress of Human Sciences at Mexico
1977	World Congress of Religious Workers, Moscow
1978	Vice-chancellors Conference, Canada
1978	Chief Guest, Vakyartha Vidvat Sadas, Sringeri
1978	United Nations University Seminar, Tokyo
1981	God Conference, MAUI, Hawaii
1982	World Congress of Religious Workers, Moscow
1983	XVIIth World Congress of Philosophy, Montreal

1983	Chairman, Unesco Meeting of Philosophers of Asia and the Pacific, Bangkok
1984	Director, International Conference on "Buddhism and National Cultures", Delhi
1985	Director, International Seminar on Śaṅkarācārya

Appendix II

Writings of K. Satchidananda Murty

English

1947	*Hinduism and Its Development*
1951	*Thought and the Divine*
1951	*The Rhythm of the Real*
1952	*Evolution of Philosophy in India* (later published as *Evolution of Indian Philosophy* in 2007)
1957	*Ṣaḍdarśana Samuccaya by Haribhadra* (Translation)
1959	*Revelation and Reason in Advaita Vedānta* (Ph.D Thesis)
1960	*The Quest for Peace* (originally published as *Studies in the Problems of Peace,* with A.C. Bouquet as Co-author)
1963	*General Education Reconsidered* (ed.)
1963	*Metaphysics, Man and Freedom*
1963	*An Exercise in Mystical Ontology*
1964	*Indian Foreign Policy*
1965	*The Indian Spirit*

1967	*Readings in Indian History, Politics and Philosophy* (ed.)
1971	*Nāgārjuna*
1972	*Current Trends in Indian Philosophy* (ed.)
1973	*The Realm of Between*
1976	*Far Eastern Philosophies*
1982	*Indian Philosophy Since 1498*
1984	*Naihsreyasa Dharma*
1985	*Philosophy in India*
1985	*The Advaitic Notion*
1989	*Radhakrishnan: His Life and Ideas* (principal author)
1991	*Ethics, Education, Indian Unity and Culture*
1993	*Vedic Hermeneutics*
1995	*The Divine Peacock: Understanding Contemporary India* (ed.)

TELUGU

1938	*Hanumad-Vijayamu*
1938	*Nama-sankirtana-mahima* (Translation of Sri Prabhudatta Brahmachari's Hindi work)
1941	*Śrīmad-Bhagavad-Gītā Savyakhyānamu*
1946	*Isopanishattu Savivaranam*
1947	*Karu Mabbulu* (Essays on Philosophical, Political and Social Problems)
1948	*Divya-Jivitamu* (Translation of Edward Leen's The Church Before Pilate)

1948	*Sri Rama Tirtha, Vedānta Darsanamu,* (Translation of vol. VI of Swami Rama Tirtha's Complete Works)
1951	*Ramanuja Darsanamu*
1959	*Pramana Paddhati Pai Prasangamu* (Translation of Descartes' *Discourse on Method* with an Introduction, and in collaboration with K.V.R. Narasimham)
1963	*Matamulu Darsanamulu* (ed.), "Religions and Philosophies", vol. VII of *Telugu Encyclopaedia* that presents in 849 pages the entire Western and Eastern philosophies and religions with contributors from all over the world)
1970	*Manishi, Mukti* (Translation of *Metaphysics, Man and Freedom*; draft by M.V.N. Swami and revised by the author)

HINDI

1962	*Samakālīn Bhāratīya Darśana* (ed.), Akhil Bharatiya Darshan Parishad

Bibliography

Primary Sources

Books by Prof. K. Satchidananda Murty

An Exercise in Mystical Ontology (Presidential Address, Akhil Bharatiya Darshana Parishad, Ninth Session), Lucknow: Lucknow University, 1963.

Current Trends in Indian Philosophy (edited with K. Ramakrishna Rao), Bombay: Asia Publishing House, 1972.

Ethics, Education, Indian Unity and Culture, Delhi: Ajanta Publications, 1991.

Evolution of Philosophy in India (A Brief Sketch), Guntur: St. Michael's Industrial School Press, 1952.

Far Eastern Philosophies, Mysore: University of Mysore, 1976.

General Education Reconsidered (ed.), Bombay: Asia Publishing House, 1963.

Hinduism and Its Development, Tenali: Sundaram and Sons, 1947.

Indian Foreign Policy, Calcutta: Scientific Book Agency, 1964.

Indian Philosophy Since 1498, Waltair: Andhra University, 1982.

Metaphysics, Man and Freedom, Waltair: Andhra University, 1963; repr. in, 1974

Nāgārjuna, Delhi: National Book Trust, 1971; repr. in 1978 and 1983.

Naihsreyasa Dharma, Varanasi: Central Institute of Higher Tibetan Studies, 1984.

Philosophy in India, Delhi: Motilal Banarsidass for Indian Council of Philosophical Research, 1985; repr. in 1991.

Radhakrishnan: His Life and Ideas (co-authored with Ashok Vohra), Delhi: Ajanta Publications, 1989.

Readings in Indian History, Politics and Philosophy (ed.), Bombay: Allied Publishers, 1967.

Revelation and Reason in Advaita Vedānta, Delhi: Motilal Banarsidass, 1974. (Originally published by Andhra University Press and Columbia University Press, 1959.)

Ṣaḍdarśana Samuccaya by Haribhadra (tr.) (*A Compendium of Six Philosophers*), New Delhi: Eastern Book Linkers, 1986. (Originally printed in 1957).

The Advaitic Notion, Sringeri: Śrī Śṛṅgerī Śāradāpīṭham, 1985; Reprinted as *The Advaitic Vision,* Bombay: Bharatiya Vidya Bhavan, 1990.

The Divine Peacock: Understanding Contemporary India (ed.), Delhi: Indian Council for Cultural Relations and Wiley Eastern, 1995.

The Indian Spirit, Waltair: Andhra University, 1965.

The Quest for Peace, Delhi: Ajanta Publications, 1986. (Originally published in 1960 as chapters in the *Studies in the Problems of Peace,* co-authored with A.C. Bouquet.)

The Realm of Between, Simla: Indian Institute of Advanced Study, 1973.

The Rhythm of the Real, Rajahmundry: Saraswati Power Press, 1951.

Thought and the Divine, Guntur: St. Michael's Industrial School Press, 1951.

Vedic Hermeneutics, New Delhi: Shri Lal Bahadur Shastri Rashtriya Sanskrit Vidyapeetha and Motilal Banarsidass, 1993.

BOOKS ON PROF. K. SATCHIDANANDA MURTY

Ramakrishna Rao, K. et al. (eds.), *Collected Criticism of K. Satchidananda Murty,* Machilipatnam: Triveni Publishers, 1975.

Sibajiban Bhattacharyya and Ashok Vohra (eds.), *The Philosophy of K. Satchidananda Murty*, New Delhi: Indian Council of Philosophical Research, 1995.

SECONDARY SOURCES

Arapura, J.G., *Radhakrishnan and Integral Experience*, Bombay: Asia Publishing House, 1966.

Bahm, Archie J., *Comparative Philosophy*, Albuquerque: World Books, 1977.

Barlingay, S.S., *Beliefs, Reasons and Reflections*, Poona: I.P.Q. Publications, 1983.

Barth, A., *The Religions of India*, Delhi: Light and Life Publishers, 1978.

Beck, Robert N. (ed.), *Perspectives in Philosophy*, New York: Holt, Rinehart and Winston, 1969.

———, *Handbook in Social Philosophy*, New York: Macmillan, 1979.

Bhattacharjee, G.P., *Evolution of Political Philosophy of M.N. Roy*. Calcutta: The Minerva Associates, 1971.

Brown, D. Mackenzie, *The White Umbrella*, Bombay: Jaico Publishing House, 1953.

Campbell, Keith, *Metaphysics: An Introduction*, California: Dickenson Publishing Company, 1976.

Chatterjee, Margaret (ed.), *Contemporary Indian Philosophy*, London: George Allen and Unwin, 1975.

———, *Philosophical Esquires*, Calcutta: New Age Publishers, 1967.

Dagobert, D. Runes, *Dictionary of Philosophy*, Anes, Lowa, Little Field: Adam and Company, 1956.

Dasgupta, S.N., *A History of Indian Philosophy*, Delhi: Motilal Banarsidass, 1975.

Durant, Will, *The Story of Philosophy*, New York: Pocket Books, 1926.

Edwards, Paul (ed.), *The Encyclopaedia of Philosophy*, New York: Macmillan and The Free Press, 1967.

Frauwalner, Erich, *History of Indian Philosophy,* Delhi: Motilal Banarsidass, 1973.

George Victor, P., *Life and Teachings of Adi Śaṅkarācārya,* Delhi: D.K. Printworld, 2002.

———, *Social Philosophy of Vedanta,* Calcutta: K.P. Bagchi and Co., 1991.

Gopal, S., *Radhakrishnan: A Biography,* Delhi: Oxford University Press, 1989.

Girija, Shaw, *Glory of Indian Culture,* New Delhi: Diamond Pocket Books, 2000.

James Hastings (ed.), *Encyclopaedia of Religion and Ethics,* Edinburgh: T & T, Clark, 1921.

Joel Feinberg, *Social Philosophy,* New Jersey: Prentice Hall, 1973.

Kennick, W.E. (ed.), *Metaphysics,* New Jersey: Prentice Hall, 1966.

Kunhan Raja, C., *Vedas,* Waltair: Andhra University, 1957.

Lal, Basantkumar, *Contemporary Indian Philosophy,* Delhi: Motilal Banarsidass, 1973.

Hiriyanna, M., *Outlines of India Philosophy,* New Delhi: George Allen & Unwin (India), 1973.

Mackenzie, J.S., *Outlines of Social Philosophy,* New York: George Allen & Unwin, 1918.

Mayer, Fredrick, *A History of Modern Philosophy,* Delhi: Eurasia Publishing House, 1966.

Michael, Aloysius, *Radhakrishnan on Hindu Moral Life and Action,* Delhi: Concept Publishing Company, 1979.

Moore, Charles A. (ed.), *The Indian Mind,* Honolulu: East-WestCenter Press, 1967.

Nagaraja Rao, P., *Fundamentals of Indian Philosophy,* New Delhi: Indian Book Company (undated).

Prabhavananda, Swami, *The Spiritual Heritage of India,* Madras: Sri Ramakrishna Matt, 1977.

Prasanna Kumar, A., *Dr. B. Pattabhi Seetharamaiah,* Waltair: Andhra University, 1978.

Radhakrishnan, S., *Indian Philosophy,* vol. II, London: George Allen Unwin, 1966.

———, *Religion in a Changing World,* London: George Allen and Unwin, 1967.

———, *The Pursuit of Truth,* Delhi: Hind Pocket Books, 1979.

Raju, P.T., *Lectures on Comparative Philosophy,* Poona: University of Poona, 1970.

Russell, Bertrand, *A History of Western Philosophy,* London: Unwin Paperbacks, 1979

Shah, Girija, *Glory of Indian Culture,* New Delhi: Diamond Pocket Books, 2000.

Sharma, C.D., *A Critical Survey of Indian Philosophy,* Delhi: Motilal Banarsidass, 1970.

Tapasyananda, Swami (tr.), *Sankara-Dig-Vijaya by Madhava-vidyaranya,* Fifth Impression, Madras: Sri Ramakrishna Math.

Thilly, Frank, *A History of Philosophy,* New York: Henry Holt and Company, 1914.

Vivekananda, Swami, *Hinduism,* Madras: Sri Ramakrishna Matt, 1980.

Wilson, H.I., *Hindu Religions,* Delhi: Bharatiya Book Corporation, 1977.

Wilson, K., *Political Philosophy of the Oppressed Indians,* Hyderabad: Book Links Corporation, 1983.

Yutang, Lin, *Wisdom of China and India,* New York: The Modern Library, 1942.

Index

PRINTWORLD